VILLAGES OF EDINBURGH:
AN ILLUSTRATED GUIDE

BY THE SAME AUTHOR

Marchmont in Edinburgh 1984
Villages of Edinburgh Volume 1 (North) 1986
Villages of Edinburgh Volume 2 (South) 1987
Edinburgh: Sciennes and the Grange 1990
Yerbury: A Photographic Collection 1850–1993 1994
Edinburgh: Gorgie and Dalry 1995
Villages of Edinburgh: An Illustrated Guide Volume 1 (North) 1997
The District of Greenbank in Edinburgh 1998

VILLAGES OF EDINBURGH:
AN ILLUSTRATED GUIDE

Volume II

Malcolm Cant

Maps by Bryan Ryalls

Foreword by
Professor Emeritus Alexander Fenton, C.B.E.

MALCOLM CANT PUBLICATIONS

First published in 1999 by
Malcolm Cant Publications
13 Greenbank Row Edinburgh EH10 5SY

ISBN 0 9526099 3 2

Typeset by Carnegie Publishing, Lancaster
Printed and bound by
Cromwell Press, Trowbridge, Wiltshire

To

my second grandchild

Kathryn

a live wire with ample energy

Contents

Foreword

I have been a Southsider ever since I came to Edinburgh in the 1950s. My first home was in Eden Lane, in a little two-roomed cottage tucked into the back of Morningside. It served as a reminder that before the spread of Edinburgh well beyond the Old Town, much of the surrounding area was farm land, with many similar single-storey buildings in the little village groupings and attached to the farms. In the south side, as in other areas, farm names are commemorated in the names of streets. More concrete evidence is also to be found, for example on the fine table tombstone in Liberton Kirkyard with its ploughing, harrowing and sowing scene of 1754. Malcolm Cant makes us very conscious of this rural underlay as we walk with him through the villages he describes.

But he also looks at the castles, mansions and big houses, at churches and schools, at the mills on the Water of Leith, at institutional buildings and places for leisure or fierce competition such as golf clubs, the Plaza Ballroom and the Dominion Cinema, at the Union Canal, and at the scene of the last public hanging in Edinburgh, in 1815 on the Braid Road. In each case, he demonstrates his profound knowledge of the City and her growth, using his awareness of the people behind the places and things as a means of bringing historical facts alive.

In my early Edinburgh days, I was a keen explorer, but I realise now, in reading these pages written by one with such expert knowledge, just how much was missed. Every reader will be inspired, as I was, to go out with this guide in hand and so gain an inner understanding of the City's development and an awareness of what history lies around us in every street and at every corner.

I have known Malcolm Cant and have experienced and enjoyed his enthusiasm for Edinburgh over many years. The City is very well served by such a son.

Professor Emeritus Alexander Fenton, C.B.E.

Acknowledgments

I am indebted to a wide range of people for their assistance in bringing this volume to fruition. They include the staff of: the Company of Merchants of the City of Edinburgh; the Edinburgh City Archivist's Department; Edinburgh University Library; the Edinburgh Room of the Central Library; Historic Scotland; the National Library of Scotland; the Royal Commission on the Ancient and Historical Monuments of Scotland; and The Scotsman Publications Ltd.

In particular areas I derived a lot of help and encouragement from the various local societies and people interested in local history. The names were included in the first edition of *Villages of Edinburgh* but the following people have also been instrumental in helping me to update the information for this volume:

COLINTON: The Argyll and Sutherland Highlanders; Maurice Berrill; Bonaly Primary School; Colinton Local History Society; Dr Ian Dugdale; Catherine H. Foggo; Lynne Gladstone-Millar; Kenneth Reid Associates; Wendy Stewart; Rev. George J. Whyte.

GILMERTON: A. Gray Muir; Rev. Dr Colin Peckham; Robbie Pentland; Rev. Donald Skinner.

JUNIPER GREEN: A. G. Boe; *Currie and Balerno News*; Mr & Mrs Downie; Eric Horberry; Rev. Bernard P. Lodge; M. R. A. Matthews; Gordon Renwick; Dr John M. Ross; Irene Thomson.

LIBERTON: Tom Addyman; William Clunie; David Gilmour; Nicholas Groves-Raines, Architects; Wilma G. H. Munro; Jean Murray; John Sanders of Simpson & Brown, Architects; Eileen Sharp; Isobel Vass; Chris Vivers; Rev. Dr John N. Young.

LONGSTONE & SLATEFORD: British Waterways; Ewan Campbell; James McKendrick; Susan Warren; Water of Leith Conservation Trust.

MORNINGSIDE: Derek Cameron; Elizabeth Casciani; Brigadier Colin Cowan; Eric Liddell Centre; Dorothy L. Forrester; A. J. Mullay;

Graham Ross; George S. Russell; St Peter's Roman Catholic School; Charles J. Smith; William R. Smith.

SWANSTON: Mr & Mrs Crawford; Robin A. Hill; Lothianburn Golf Club; Mr & Mrs McLagan; John Percival; Swanston Golf Club.

I am also indebted to Bryan Ryalls for the clear and informative maps of the various locations. Photographs are acknowledged throughout the text. John and Val Tuckwell undertook the editorial work; Oula Jones compiled the index and read the proofs; Neville Moir steered the whole project through the design and printing stages to the finished book; and James Hutcheson designed the book cover. I also thank Gordon Wright of Gordon Wright Publishing for giving me permission to quote from *The Place Names of Edinburgh* by Stuart Harris.

I would also like to thank Professor Emeritus Alexander Fenton, C.B.E., Director of the European Ethnological Research Centre, or Sandy as he is more commonly known, for writing the Foreword and for his continuing interest in this project, among many others.

Finally, I thank my wife Phyllis, and our extended family, who have always been on hand for a host of tasks associated with the book.

Malcolm Cant F.C.I.I., F.S.A.(Scot.)

Introduction

I first made a study of some of the surviving village communities in Edinburgh in the mid-1980s. The result of that research was published for me by John Donald Publishers Ltd., of Edinburgh in two volumes as *Villages of Edinburgh*, which have now been out of print for some time. Recently I looked through my research notes again and revisited the places which had occupied so much of my time more than a decade ago. I discovered that time had not, in fact, stood still and that important changes had taken place. When I contacted the various local societies and history groups I was very favourably impressed by the amount of work which had been undertaken in gathering slides and prints, and recording the history of each locality. Much more information had come to light since I was last involved and major conservation projects have ensured the survival of important historical buildings, including Mackenzie's Cottage at Colinton and Liberton Tower and Liberton House.

After studying all the villages again I decided to update my information and alter my style to present *Villages of Edinburgh: an Illustrated Guide*. In doing this I hope to encourage my readers, not only to enjoy the book at home, but to visit these village communities and actually walk the route. With that in mind I have arranged the script topographically, supported by a much wider selection of photographs depicting the main places of interest. A detailed street map, with the relevant places marked, has also been included at the beginning of each chapter. In addition, a general map of Edinburgh appears at the beginning of the book showing the location of the villages included in each volume. All the villages can be reached by car, but, in this enlightened age, my recommendation is to use public transport where possible.

In the first volume of *Villages of Edinburgh: an Illustrated Guide*, published in 1997, I concentrated on the villages in what might be described as the northern hemisphere of the city, which included Corstorphine, Cramond, Davidson's Mains, Dean, Duddingston,

Newhaven, Restalrig and Stockbridge. In the second volume I deal with the villages on the south side, namely Colinton, Gilmerton, Juniper Green, Liberton, Longstone and Slateford, Morningside and Swanston.

Malcolm Cant F.C.I.I., F.S.A. (Scot.)

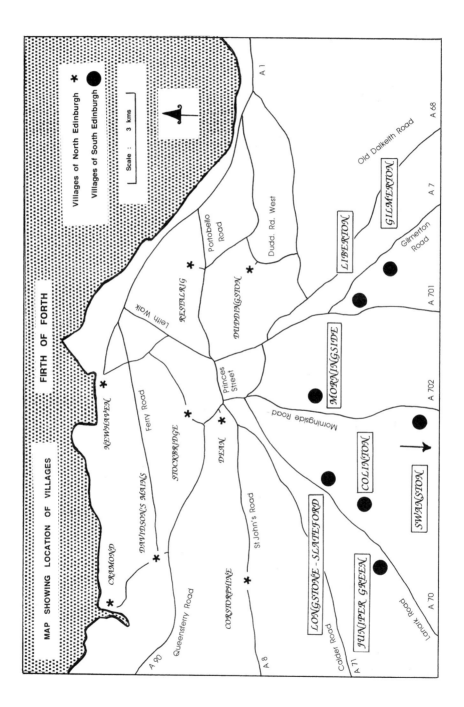

MAP SHOWING LOCATION OF VILLAGES

FIRTH OF FORTH

Villages of North Edinburgh ✱
Villages of South Edinburgh ●

Scale : 3 kms

CRAMOND

NEWHAVEN

DAVIDSON'S MAINS

Queensferry Road

A 90

Ferry Road

STOCKBRIDGE

Leith Walk

RESTALRIG

Portobello Road

DEAN

Princes Street

DUDDINGSTON

Dudd. Rd. West

A 1

CORSTORPHINE

St John's Road

A 8

Morningside Road

MORNINGSIDE

LIBERTON

A 702

A 701

A 7

GILMERTON

Gilmerton Road

Old Dalkeith Road

A 68

Calder Road

A 71

LONGSTONE - SLATEFORD

JUNIPER GREEN

Lanark Road

A 70

COLINTON

SWANSTON

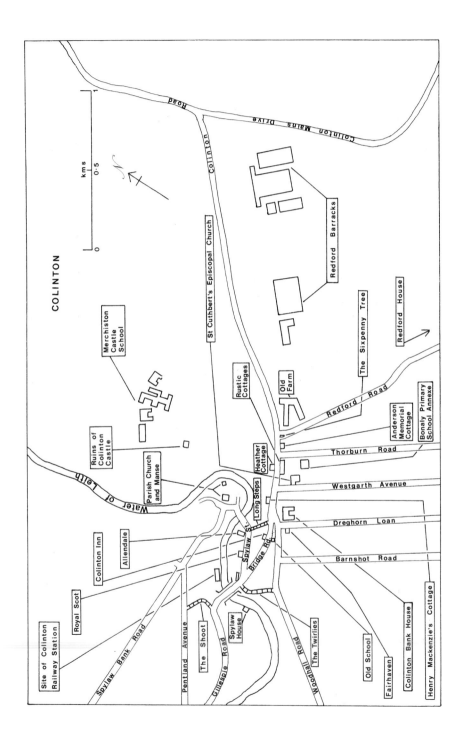

COLINTON

kms
0   0.5   1

Site of Colinton Railway Station
Royal Scot
Colinton Inn
Allendale
Spylaw Bank Road
Pentland Avenue
The Shoot
Gillespie Road
Spylaw House
Woodhall Road
The Twirlies
Old School
Fairhaven
Colinton Bank House
Henry Mackenzie's Cottage

Water of Leith
Ruins of Colinton Castle
Parish Church and Manse
Merchiston Castle School

Spylaw St
Long Steps
Bridge Rd
Heather Cottage
Rustic Cottages
Old Farm
St Cuthbert's Episcopal Church

Dreghorn Loan
Westgarth Avenue
Barnshot Road
Thorburn Road

Anderson Memorial Cottage
Bonaly Primary School Annexe
Redford Road
The Sixpenny Tree
Redford House
Redford Barracks
Colinton Mains Drive
Colinton Road

CHAPTER ONE

Colinton

Colinton village lies in the valley of the Water of Leith approximately five miles south-west of Princes Street. From the city centre the usual route is by Lothian Road and Home Street, turning right at the King's Theatre and continuing out of town by way of Polwarth, Craiglockhart and Firrhill. At Firrhill, the main road to Colinton turns right and passes Redford Barracks, built prior to the First World War by Colin Macandrew & Partners Ltd., public works contractors, of Edinburgh.

Colinton grew up around the ancient church of Halis (Hailes) which is believed to have existed as early as the eleventh century. The village was originally settled around the Water of Leith where the natural water course was used to power the mill machinery. Like many similar rural communities nearby, its lifestyle was hardly affected by Edinburgh until the latter half of the nineteenth century. However, with the advent of public transport services by rail and by road, considerable expansion took place at the turn of the century, particularly around Woodhall Road and Spylaw Bank Road. Widespread bungalow development occurred before the Second World War, followed by an almost continuous building programme since the 1950s. Despite this rapid growth in the surrounding population, the old village has remained the unchallenged focal point of the community.

The main places of interest in the village can be reached on foot, although the terrain is fairly steep in parts. For those keen to travel further afield, there are several interesting walks, including the monuments in Redford Road and what remains of the mills on the banks of the Water of Leith. A useful guide is *Colinton: Seven Walks* first published by the Colinton Amenity Association in 1985, which can be bought in the village shops.

No. 9 electric tram entering the single-track section opposite Inchdrewar
House on the Colinton route in 1926. *From the D.L.G. Hunter Collection.
Photographed by the late E.O. Catford.*

THE VILLAGE WALK

The village walk usually begins at the junction of Colinton Road and Redford Road, where a young sapling, in the centre of the traffic island, struggles to live up to the memory of its ancient predecessor, the Sixpenny Tree. It is said that the old tree, not long removed, marked the spot where the members of the Guild of Papermakers met to debate the issues of the day, and to pay their dues of sixpence each into a common fund. West of the new Sixpenny Tree, on the east corner of Thorburn Road, is the Lady Rowand Anderson Memorial Cottage which has a skewed date stone at ground-floor level, giving the year of construction, 1922, and the initials of Lady Rowand Anderson and her husband, Sir Robert Rowand Anderson, the architect. Behind the Memorial Cottage are the Colinton Cottage Homes, a sheltered housing complex, started in 1889, and run by the Aged Christian Friend Society of Scotland. Another famous architect, operating in Colinton and

The Craiglockhart to Colinton bus at Redford Barracks in September 1920. Redford Barracks were designed by Harry B. Measures and built by Colin Macandrew & Partners of Edinburgh between 1909 and 1915.
From the D.L.G. Hunter Collection. Photographed by the late E.O. Catford.

The Household Cavalry leave Redford Barracks for Princes Street during the State visit of the King and Queen of Norway to Edinburgh in 1994.

beyond, was Sir Robert S. Lorimer who designed Rustic Cottages, with the distinctive boat-shaped dormers, on the main road between Thorburn Road and Westgarth Avenue. Opposite Rustic Cottages is Heather Cottage, built around 1810 as part of Colinton House estate. Its gables, raised above the line of the slates, and the dripstones at the base of the chimneys, confirm that this quaint old cottage was once thatched.

The east corner of Westgarth Avenue is occupied by St Cuthbert's Church, opened on 10th August 1889 after six years' campaigning and fund-raising by the Episcopalian population of Colinton and its surrounding districts. The salient dates in its history are recorded in *An Act of Faith* written by Wendy Stewart at the time of the centenary in 1989. Recent research undertaken by Dr Ian Dugdale has also established that from 1883 to 1889, when the church was opened, the congregation worshipped in the building known as Allandale at the foot of Spylaw Street. Prior to Dr Dugdale's research it was assumed that the early meetings had been held in the Liberal Reading Room (on the site of the present-day John Menzies shop in Bridge Road) and in the Iron Hall which preceded the present Loan Hall in Dreghorn Loan. The Westgarth Avenue corner site was offered by Robert Andrew Macfie at a nominal feu duty of a peppercorn, and work was started

St Cuthbert's Episcopal Church, Westgarth Avenue, designed by Rowand Anderson, and opened on 10th August 1889 by Bishop Dowden.

in October 1888 with a substantial grant from the Walker Trust. The building was completed in May 1889 and opened by Bishop Dowden on 10th August 1889. The external appearance of the church has been radically, but skilfully, altered over the years. In 1893 Rowand Anderson completed the tower with a lead-covered belfry instead of the intended spire, and the following year the new south transept was formed containing the Lady Chapel and the organ chamber. The church hall was added to the south in 1922, but it was not until 1934 that the church took on its present-day appearance. Rowand Anderson's original four-bay nave was expertly lengthened by the addition of three bays to the west, no external trace of this being obvious in the exactly matched stonework. The roof structure and the Ailsa Craig granite floor were also repeated to create a unified interior. Internally, the appearance of the church is at once joyful, yet dignified. The nave has

The entrance to Colinton village *c.* 1870 with Colinton School behind the trees on the left. The Rev. Lewis Balfour (grandfather of Robert Louis Stevenson) was minister at Colinton from 1823 until his death in 1860. The photograph shows Colinton as R.L.S. would have known it before he left Edinburgh in 1887. *Courtesy of the late Miss E.D. Robertson.*

a central aisle, flanked by pews donated in memory of the church's many benefactors, and the baptistry contains a magnificent font with an ornate cone-shaped cover finely counter-balanced so that it can be raised easily to reveal the baptismal bowl. The stained glass work includes: on the north side a window to St Cuthbert; on the east, three windows depicting the Resurrection; on the west, a commemorative window to the Riddells of Craiglockhart; and in the south transept, windows dedicated to Our Lady, Saint Cuthbert and Saint George.

Immediately west of St Cuthbert's Episcopal Church two starkly contrasting buildings reinforce Colinton's literary connections. Thomas Murray, author of *Biographical Annals of the Parish of Colinton*, lived for a time in Colinton Bank House, the imposing villa perched on the high ground between the bottom of Westgarth Avenue and Dreghorn Loan. Opposite Colinton Bank House a square pillar, with a small bronze plaque, stood outside Henry Mackenzie's Cottage. After many years of neglect the building was almost derelict before being saved. During 1995 all that remained were two gable ends wrapped in blue polythene and supported by temporary scaffolding. By the end of 1996 the cottage had been fully restored by the architect, Ron Galloway and the builder, J. Gunn, and was reopened by Malcolm Rifkind, M.P. on 3rd March 1997. A time capsule, containing a copy of the architect's drawings and other artefacts, was placed in a hole in the wall of the new gable, and the commemorative plaque was repositioned on the exterior wall of the renovated building:

IN THIS HOUSE LIVED
HENRY MACKENZIE
AUTHOR OF
THE MAN OF FEELING
BORN 25TH AUGUST 1745
DIED 14TH JANUARY 1831

As we proceed down into the village, the Long Steps on the right give access to Colinton Parish Church, but the short section of steps which led up to Woodhall Road was removed in 1982 owing to the danger to pedestrians crossing Bridge Road. A small stone, which can be seen from Woodhall Road, was erected marking the line of the right of way:

THIS STONE MARKS THE LINE
OF THE ANCIENT ROUTE FROM THE PENTLAND HILLS
TO THE FORD AND OLD BRIDGE
OVER THE WATER OF LEITH

Another flight of steps comes down from Woodhall Road at the large square building on the left, built as Colinton Public School, and subsequently used for a while as Colinton Public Library. Looking at the austere building today it is difficult to imagine that in 1843 Robert Hunter was employed at a salary of £34 per annum, plus £40 in fees, to teach one hundred pupils English, writing, geometry, arithmetic and geography – in addition to his other duties as session clerk, clerk to the heritors, postmaster, and collector of parochial assessments. Even assuming that he had assistance from other class teachers, there must have been occasions when he wished that the blunt, but salutary motto, believed to have been above the previous school building, had been transferred to the new school: AUT DISCE, AUT DOCE, AUT ABI – learn, teach or go away. Colinton can trace the history of its schools back to the mid-seventeenth century when rather rudimentary accommodation was available in the parochial school beside the parish church. Up until 1663 the children were taught in the church building. By 1811 the Kirk Session Records show that the old school building was too ruinous to be repaired, which led to the construction of the 1815 building. There was also a smaller 'female and infants' school built in 1870 on the south-west corner of Dreghorn Loan and Woodhall Road. In 1891 Colinton's first Board School was opened in Thorburn Road and served as the district school until a new Colinton School was built in Redford Place in 1967. Bonaly Primary School was opened in 1976 and the Thorburn Road building was used for the Infant Department.

The Hut or G. L. Miller's fruit store in Bridge Road, the site of which was later occupied by Harwells of Colinton and later by John Menzies, booksellers and newsagents.

Mary Thorburn, postwoman of Colinton, in 1916.

It is possible to reach Colinton Parish Church by the Long Steps but that route cuts off the remainder of Bridge Road and Spylaw Street, both of which form an integral part of the village. The shops with houses above, a few yards down from the Colinton Inn, were built as Janefield in 1879 for £2000 by Mrs Jane Johnston, the postmistress of Colinton. Prior to 1900 the two shop units next to the Colinton Inn housed the Colinton Dance Hall, also known as Johnston's Ballroom. By 1911 the Johnston family owned and let out twenty (out of a total of thirty-one) retail outlets in the village, including the line of single-storey shops farther down Bridge Road. Adjacent to Janefield are two houses built around 1810 in the form of pedimented lodges. At the head of Cuddies Lane the building in warm rustic brick occupies the site of a small petrol station which belonged to Waddell of Colinton whose ancestors owned the smiddy on the same site. In those days

The Argyll & Sutherland Highlanders marching up Spylaw Street after attending Colinton Parish Church in the early 1950s. The regimental mascot, Cruachan, a Shetland Pony, leads the parade in Bridge Road.

there were no steps in Cuddies Lane and the horses were able to enter from either the top or the bottom of the lane. Many Colinton residents will recall the detached two-storey building on the south side as the village post office, now a dental surgery. Few citizens, however, will remember when the building was occupied by Harry Blyth, the butcher, who kept live chickens in open boxes at the door to enable his customers to select their Christmas dinner. At the foot of Bridge Road the viaduct, recently strengthened, carries the main road over the valley of the Water of Leith to Juniper Green and Wester Hailes. Before the bridge was built the old village street turned abruptly into Spylaw Street which still retains many interesting links with earlier days. In the building abutting the bridge parapet Colinton's first telephone exchange was housed in the large front room on the first floor. The adjacent, two-storey building with the redbrick facings was the County Roadman's house, the Colinton man, William Robertson, occupying the upper floor, and the Juniper Green man, Peter Stenhouse, occupying the lower floor. Completing the trio was No. 24, formerly Darwal, the village police station. On the south side of Spylaw Street, opposite the Royal Scot (previously the Railway Inn), is a long row of pantiled cottages with timber porches over the pavement. In recent years they have been renovated under the direction of the Merchant Company Endowments Trust. At the foot of the hill Laurel Bank and Allendale (previously spelt Allandale) look out onto what was the heart of the village beside the ford, the old bridge, the school, the mill and the parish church.

On the far side of the single-arch bridge a church has stood on or near the present Colinton Parish Church for at least nine hundred years. To commemorate its foundation many special events were organised by the church in 1995, and *The Colinton Story* by Lynne Gladstone-Millar was published, giving a very scholarly account of this ancient parish. A brief history of the early foundation of the church was compiled by the Rev. William Lockhart D.D., minister of the parish from 1861 to 1902, and inscribed in 1895 on a wooden board which hangs inside the entrance porch:

ST CUTHBERT'S CHURCH & PARISH
OF HALIS, NOW COLINTON
WERE FOUNDED ABOUT THE YEAR
1095

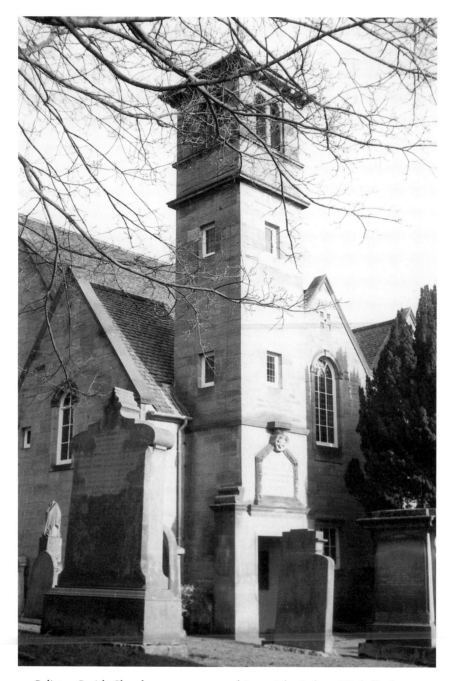

Colinton Parish Church was reconstructed in 1908 by Sydney Mitchell who rearranged the gables and re-used the square tower from the old church on the same site. *Photograph by Phyllis M. Cant.*

BY
PRINCE ETHELRED
THIRD SON OF
MALCOLM III AND QUEEN MARGARET
AND BROTHER OF
EDGAR, ALEXANDER I AND DAVID I
KINGS OF SCOTLAND

THE ANCIENT CHURCH, WHICH PROBABLY TOOK THE
PLACE OF AN OLDER PICTISH, BRITISH OR SAXON
FOUNDATION WAS DEDICATED ON THE
27TH SEPTEMBER 1248
IT DISAPPEARED ABOUT THE YEAR 1560 OR WAS
PROBABLY DESTROYED DURING THE EARL OF
HERTFORD'S INVASION IN 1544–45 IN THE REIGN
OF HENRY VIII
ANOTHER CHURCH WAS PLACED HERE CIRCA
1636
IN THE REIGN OF CHARLES I

WILLIAM LOCKHART D.D. 1895

The building in its present form dates only from 1908. The church to which Dr Lockhart refers was replaced in 1771 by Robert Weir, mason, and William Watters, wright, working to their own designs, with further improvements in 1837 by the architect, David Bryce. In 1908 a major reconstruction was done by Sydney Mitchell who rearranged the gables and reused Bryce's square tower over the new entrance porch. A sundial inscribed SIR JAMES FOULLES 1630 was incorporated on the external angle of the porch. The interior, redesigned in 1908, is a pleasing combination of pink sandstone pillars, dark woodwork and pastel-coloured plaster. The nave, entered under the organ and choir gallery at the west end, closes with a finely proportioned apse at the east end, flanked on either side by galleries. The pulpit is placed on the left, above which is an oak cross-beam inscribed O WORSHIP THE LORD IN THE BEAUTY OF HOLINESS. Natural light to the apse is admitted through nine windows designed and executed by James Ballantyne, depicting the Fruits of the Spirit – Love, Joy, Peace, Patience, Kindness, Goodness, Fidelity, Gentleness and Self Control.

In October 1998 a new two-storey building, incorporating a new entrance to the church, was opened by Lord Provost Eric Milligan. The upper, or churchyard level, provides a large foyer giving access to the church, a function room known as the Dell Room, the Hailes Vestry and other offices. The lower, or courtyard level, incorporates the Woodhall Room, the Bonaly Room and the Redford Room.

The south aisle of the church contains the oldest surviving stone from the graveyard:

> HEIR LYIS ANE
> HONORABIL VO
> MAN A HIRIOT
> SPOVS TO I FOVLIS
> OF COLLING TOVN
> VAS QVHA DIED
> AVGVST 1593

Some of the stones, of equal interest, though not of equal antiquity, have suffered badly from the weather in the old graveyard which surrounds the church on all four sides. Colinton Churchyard abounds with interest and requires more than one visit for a comprehensive review. Two seventeenth-century stones, near the south-west angle of the church, for Thomsone 1678 and Denholm 1696, have lost much of their original detail, but the skull, crossbones and cherubs for farmer Ferguson 1771 can still be seen against the east gable of the gatehouse. On the north side of the church a line of imposing tombs forms the boundary between the old graveyard and a later extension. Among these is the pedimented mausoleum of one of Colinton's most famous residents, James Gillespie of Spylaw, who died on 8th April 1797. To the east is the family burial place of Dr Lewis Balfour, minister of the parish from 1823 to 1860, maternal grandfather of Robert Louis Stevenson. A more recent family stone is in memory of Lt. Cdr. David Ian Balfour R.N., killed in action aboard H.M.S. *Sheffield* in the Falklands in 1982.

Many other stones have been researched but so far no one appears to have traced the epitaph, believed to have been on a Colinton stone, for which the author David Shankie searched in vain:

> Here lyes the banes o' Cuthbert Denholm
> If ye saw him noo ye wouldna ken him!

Colinton Manse lies at a lower level from the old graveyard, on the banks of the Water of Leith. It was built in 1784 by Robert Weir but has been altered on numerous occasions, notably in the post-Robert Louis Stevenson period when the entrance doorway was moved to the south wall from its previous position facing the church.

At this point the Colinton walk leaves the parish church and proceeds up the very steep Spylaw Bank Road to Lanark Road. Alternatively, it is possible to take the path through Colinton Dell to Slateford. Some of the places of interest on the Dell route, for example, Boag's Mill, Redhall House and Jinkaboot, are dealt with in Chapter 5 on Longstone and Slateford.

Meantime, at No. 52 Spylaw Bank Road, the harled and red sandstone dwellings enclosing a central fountain are the Sir William Fraser Homes, established by a bequest of £25,000 from Sir William Fraser, K.C.B., LL.D. (1816–1898), a noted genealogist and Deputy Keeper of the Records of Scotland. These homes for the elderly, designed by the architect Arthur Balfour Paul and opened in 1901, are now administered by the Merchant Company Endowments Trust. From Pentland Avenue access through a narrow lane and a flight of steps known as The Shoot leads back to Colinton viaduct, below which is a small cairn marking the site of Colinton Station, on a spur line of the Caledonian Railway between Slateford and Balerno. Nothing remains of the track, sidings or station buildings but the track bed is part of the Water of Leith Walkway. Under the arches of the viaduct, beside the ground display of mill wheels, a flight of steps leads to

L.M.S. 15210 at Colinton Station on 30th October 1943 on the last day of passenger service. *From the D. L. G. Hunter Collection.*

James Gillespie of Spylaw, snuff manufacturer, on the left, and his brother John who ran the retail business in the High Street of Edinburgh. *From* Kay's Original Portraits.

Spylaw Public Park and Spylaw House, now subdivided into private flats. Spylaw House was built in 1773 for James Gillespie beside an earlier house of about 1650 in which the snuff factory was established. James and his brother John remained bachelors all their days. John looked after the retail shop in the High Street in Edinburgh while James lived at Spylaw House superintending the snuff mill. Frugal and industrious by nature, but not miserly, James acquired great wealth from the business, though he never ceased to live on close and amicable terms with his employees and his tenants. Gillespie had many of the trappings of wealth, including a carriage with the initials J G on the side, which prompted the Hon. Henry Erskine to suggest, rather facetiously, that the carriage should bear the motto:

> Wha wad hae thocht it,
> That noses had bocht it.

When Gillespie died in 1797 he left a vast fortune for the endowment

Carts, full of children, are ready to move off from Dreghorn Loan on the
Colinton Parish Church Sunday School trip in 1909.

of a hospital for aged men and women and a free school for boys.
Gillespie's Hospital was erected in 1802 in Gillespie Crescent on the
site of the old mansionhouse of Wrychtishousis near Bruntsfield.

At the village end of the viaduct, the steps known locally as The
Twirlies go up to Woodhall Road which leads back to the head of
Bridge Road. Until recently the old school building was occupied as
the doctors' surgery which was transferred in 1986 to a new building
near the Telephone Exchange in Colinton Road. The villa called
Fairhaven at the foot of Dreghorn Loan occupies the site of the
female and infants school, demolished when the Thorburn Road school
was built.

THE CASTLES AND MANSIONS

Colinton had an unusually high number of castles and mansions, many
of which still remain, albeit greatly altered from the original.

Colinton Castle and Colinton House

The ruins of the once famous Colinton Castle, home of the Foulis
family of Colinton, stand on the north side of Colinton Road, east of

the junction with Redford Road, in the private grounds of what is now
Merchiston Castle School. According to Small's *Castles and Mansions
of the Lothians*, Colinton Castle dates from *c*.1450, although the Royal
Commission on the Ancient and Historical Monuments of Scotland, in
its 10th Report, dates the castle not earlier than the sixteenth century.
Whatever the exact age of the castle, there is no doubt that the Foulis
family had a significant presence in Colinton in the early sixteenth
century when they acquired the smaller baronies of Dreghorn, Baads
(around Fordel Cottage), and Oxgangs.

Several members of the Foulis family were distinguished members of
the Scottish judiciary. Sir James Foulis, King's Advocate in 1527, was
appointed a member of the College of Justice at its institution in 1532.
A later member of the family, also Sir James, became a Senator of the
College of Justice in 1661 as Lord Colinton, followed by his son, who
was raised to the bench in 1674 as Lord Reidford or Redford. Despite
holding high office the family was not without its problems. Following
the occupation of the castle by Cromwell's troops in 1650 the Foulis
family sustained crippling financial losses. Damage to houses, barns,
byres, corn and stock, particularly at the Mains of Colinton, was so
great that large sections of the estate, Dreghorn, Craiglockhart and
Comiston, had to be sold to recoup the losses. Towards the end of the
eighteenth century part of the estate of Colinton, and the castle, were
sold by the Foulis's to the famous banker William Forbes of Pitsligo.

At the present day Colinton Castle is an ivy-covered ruin bereft of
almost all its original features. The oldest part of the castle, probably
three storeys in height, was rectangular in shape, measuring 74 by 26
feet, with its long walls running east to west. The original staircase
was in the south wall, but when the new wing was added to the north
in the seventeenth century, the opportunity was taken to incorporate
a new staircase in the angle between the old and new buildings.

When Sir William Forbes took over the estate in 1800 his first idea,
after discussion with John Fraser, mason and architect in Colinton,
was to repair and extend Colinton Castle. Plans were produced, but
another team of architects, headed by Thomas Harrison, was busy
preparing plans for a completely new house which was started in 1801
and completed in 1806. The new Colinton House was in stark contrast
to the old castle. Craigleith ashlar was used extensively in the broad
five-bay frontage, reached through a central porch of coupled Ionic

Merchiston Castle School in Colinton Road was designed by Norman A. Dick and W. J. Walker Todd.

columns. Fortunately the style and texture of the new stone was so different to the castle that it escaped at least the worst excesses of plunder. Unfortunately in 1804 the roof of the castle was deliberately removed in a 'well intentioned' bid to create a picturesque ruin. Sir William died in 1806 as the house was nearing completion but before he had taken formal possession of it. It was an untimely end for a man who, by his own efforts, had risen from being a poor orphan to become the principal of the banking company, Forbes Hunter & Co. of Edinburgh. One of his sons later disposed of the estate to the first Lord Dunfermline, Speaker of the House of Commons from 1835 to 1839, who spent his retirement at Colinton House until his death in 1858 at the age of eighty. Thereafter the estate passed to his son Sir Ralph Abercromby K.C.B. (the second Lord Dunfermline), whose only child, a daughter, married Major John Moubray Trotter.

Since 1930 Colinton Castle and Colinton House have formed part of the policies of Merchiston Castle School, the origin of which can be found more than a century earlier in central Edinburgh. In 1828 Charles Chalmers, brother of Dr Thomas Chalmers, the famous leader of the Disruption of 1843, lived at Park Place near Bristo, the site of which is now occupied by the McEwan Hall. He moved there to obtain more space for his university student boarders to whom he taught mathematics and science, but within a short time he was again in need of larger premises. He obtained a lease of the old Merchiston Tower on the Borough Muir (at one time the home of John Napier, inventor of logarithms) and moved there in 1833 with about thirty boys to establish Merchiston Castle Academy. Chalmers remained headmaster and owner of the school until 1850, when he was followed by John Gibson from 1850 to 1856 and then by Thomas Harvey from 1856 to 1863. By then the school had been established for thirty years but greater continuity was achieved on the appointment of John Johnston Rogerson who remained as headmaster for thirty-five years. Under Rogerson, or 'the Chief' as he became known, Merchiston 'advanced in number and renown', particularly as the City of Edinburgh extended from Tollcross. Towards the end of his term of office, Rogerson ensured the continuity of the school by making it a private company in 1896.

At the end of the First World War, Merchiston entered a decade of hectic activity, precipitated by the simple but laudable aim of providing a memorial to the 176 boys and masters who had been killed in action. By 1922 the architect N. A. Dick had completed plans for a Memorial Hall, but although the plans were approved by the Dean of Guild Court, it refused permission to build. Colinton Road was very narrow and a Memorial Hall abutting the roadway would prevent any road-widening scheme in the future. Suddenly the directors were faced with a greater problem than building the War Memorial. The school was hemmed in on all sides by residential development; there was no possibility of expansion; and its playing fields in Colinton Road were also under threat. Fortunately Colinton House came on the market and was acquired in October 1924, with financial assistance from the sale of Merchiston Tower to the Merchant Company of Edinburgh, along with the playing fields set aside for the new George Watson's College building. W. J. Walker Todd and Norman A. Dick were employed as architects for the new Merchiston Castle School in the grounds of Colinton House.

Dreghorn Castle

Dreghorn Castle was one of Colinton's grandest houses, probably built originally by Sir William Murray, Master of Works to King Charles II

(1630–1685). It lay amid extensive wooded policies entirely hidden from view between what is now Redford Loan and the City Bypass. Of the castle nothing remains, but two lodge houses are still extant: one lies beside the bridge across the Braid Burn south of Dreghorn Loan; and the other forms part of a modern villa development in Oxgangs Road North a few hundred yards north of Hunters Tryst. A third, beside the old bridge in Redford Road, was demolished many years ago.

The castle was home to a long list of influential people over the centuries. Towards the end of the seventeenth century it belonged to David Pitcairn who is buried in Colinton Kirkyard. After the death of David Pitcairn in 1709, his son sold the property, in 1717, to George Home of Kello W.S., Town Clerk of Edinburgh during the time that his father was Lord Provost from 1698 to 1700. During the remainder of the eighteenth century there were four owners, two of whom resided at Dreghorn for a few years only: 1735–1754 Robert Dalrymple W.S; 1754–1760 Dr Andrew St. Clair, Professor of Medicine at Edinburgh University; 1760–1764 George Dempster of Dunnichen and Skibo; 1764–1796 John Maclaurin (Lord Dreghorn), author of several books including a valuable *Essay on Copyright*. In a caustic review of Lord Dreghorn's poetical efforts, Dr Thomas Murray commented that Volume 1 of the *Works of Lord Dreghorn* consisted of his poems 'or rather verses that rhyme'. In 1797 Dreghorn Castle was bought by Alexander Trotter, paymaster to the Royal Navy, and remained in the possession of the Trotters for three generations. During this era, but probably nearer to 1820, large-scale alterations gave the castle its distinctive castellated appearance. The Trotters' involvement with Dreghorn came to an end when Mr Coutts Trotter, grandson of Alexander Trotter, disposed of the estate around 1871. The new owner was R. A. Macfie of the famous sugar-refining family whose father John Macfie came from Greenock in 1804 to expand the business in Elbe Street, Leith. In 1810 John Macfie married Alison Thorburn, daughter of William Thorburn merchant of Leith, and R. A. Macfie was born in 1811. After schooling in Leith and Edinburgh he attended Edinburgh University and then spent two years in a Leith merchant's office. Later he joined his father's sugar refinery business in Leith and also spent several years in Glasgow and Liverpool. After a long business career, combined with a close association with the Liberals under Gladstone, R. A. Macfie retired to Dreghorn where he became a prominent member of the Colinton community. As a member of the Colinton School Board he was closely involved in 1891 in the building of the new Colinton School in Thorburn Road, the street being named after his mother. He died on 16th February 1893 and was buried in South Leith Churchyard in the family grave.

During the early part of the twentieth century, Dreghorn Castle was used as a private school, after which it was acquired by the War Department. Access to the grounds by the public was effectively discouraged by several signs, strategically placed, bearing the portentous message: DANGER SOLDIERS USE BOMBS HERE WHICH CAN KILL YOU: DON'T TOUCH ANYTHING: IT MAY EXPLODE. Explode it did, but not accidentally. In the early 1950s the War Department found that the castle was superfluous to their requirements and that a prohibitive sum of money would be required to remedy the effects of poor maintenance, vandalism and dry rot. Reluctantly a decision was taken to demolish the old building, after salvaging the lead and three ancient stone plaques bearing coats of arms. In April 1955, the 300 Parachute Squadron Royal Engineers T.A. moved in and with the use of flame throwers reduced the building to a desolate shell. On Sunday 1st May 1955 they returned

The seventeenth-century Dreghorn Castle, built by Sir William Murray, Master of Works to King Charles II, was demolished in April 1955. *From* Views of Juniper Green and District.

with explosives and razed the castle to the ground – three centuries of history gone in a matter of seconds. The three armorial stones have not been traced. No part of the structure remains, although a solitary baluster, perhaps with its own story to tell, adorns the front garden of a bungalow in Redford Loan.

Redford House

Although Redford House dates from about the same period as Dreghorn Castle (mid-seventeenth century), its more modest design has enabled it to adapt more easily to change. It lies in private grounds to the north of the broad section of Redford Road, near the junction with Redford Avenue.

The name Redford came to prominence in 1674 when the eldest son of Sir James Foulis (Lord Colinton), the Lord Justice Clerk, was raised to the bench and took the title Lord Reidford. By 1712 Redford was in the possession of George Haliburton, Lord Provost of Edinburgh from 1740 to 1742. He sold it in 1740 to John Young, a brewer in Edinburgh whose daughter, Mrs Allen, succeeded to it on his death. Mrs Allen's grandson, James Allen, was born at Redford in 1771, and distinguished himself in medicine and literature. At the end of the eighteenth century the estate was acquired by Alexander Trotter of Dreghorn and later by R. A. Macfie.

Although R. A. Macfie was not perhaps the most distinguished owner of Redford, he was certainly the most imaginative, spending large sums of money in acquiring ornamental stonework from the Royal Infirmary in Edinburgh. The first Royal Infirmary, designed by William Adam, was built in 1738 on a site later occupied by South Bridge School in Infirmary Street. Although additional accommodation was provided in 1853 for surgical patients, the medical hospital continued in the original 1738 building. In 1866 a decision was taken to rehouse both the surgical and medical hospitals in a new building at Lauriston designed by David Bryce, and opened on 29th October 1879. The 1738 building lay unoccupied for several years after Lauriston was opened, but when it was demolished in 1884 R. A. Macfie of Dreghorn put in a successful bid for most of the ornamental stonework. He deployed the stonework in a number of interesting schemes, most of which are intact today.

Perhaps the most ambitious of them was the removal of the central

The Covenanters' Monument in Redford Road, constructed under the
direction of R. A. Macfie out of columns from the old Royal Infirmary which
was demolished *c.* 1884. *Photograph by Phyllis M. Cant.*

pediment above the main doorway, consisting of three bays, or windows, flanked by massive leafy scrolls, one depicting thistles and the other roses. This very heavy masonry was built into the south wall of the stable block at Redford House, and Ionic pilasters and a niche with the inscription GEORGIUS II REX were built into the west wall. The niche is empty, however, as the statue of George II was retained by the Infirmary and placed in the forecourt of the new building in Lauriston Place. In the mid-1960s the stable block at Redford was renovated to create living accommodation, without altering the old scrolls, which can still be seen through a high boundary fence on Redford Road.

Within a hundred yards of the scrolls, near the entrance to Dreghorn Barracks, another of Macfie's transplants from the Infirmary has given new life to a group of four Ionic pillars taken from a colonnade in front of the old medical building. These pillars were re-erected in their present position in 1885, primarily to commemorate the Covenanters, although other historical references appear high up on the square entablature: ROMANS; CROMWELL 1650; COVENANTERS 1666; CHARLES 1745. On a rough-hewn stone nearby are several stirring verses beginning:

> A people of whose line was Patrick born
> Whose record Wallace Knox and Watt adorn
> Whose patriots, heroes, martyrs true and bold
> On fairest page of history are enrolled.

The third link with the old Infirmary is temporarily in store. It consists of a large ornamental plaque, with a lengthy inscription commemorating General Gordon which was on the front wall of an isolated house, Fordel Cottage. The cottage stood on the south side of Redford Road a few yards west of the Dreghorn Link from the City Bypass. In recent years the cottage was well kept with substantial timber fencing enclosing a well-tended vegetable garden, but it became unoccupied during construction of the Bypass. Its demolition in 1985 removed the last link with the hamlet of Fordel described in W. B. Robertson's *Pictures of Colinton in the early Twentieth Century*. Mr Robertson illustrates three houses: Fordel Cottage, at one time the gamekeeper's cottage for Dreghorn estate; a cottage with a pantiled roof used as a military post office by the army during the First World War; and a smaller thatched cottage used by an estate gardener.

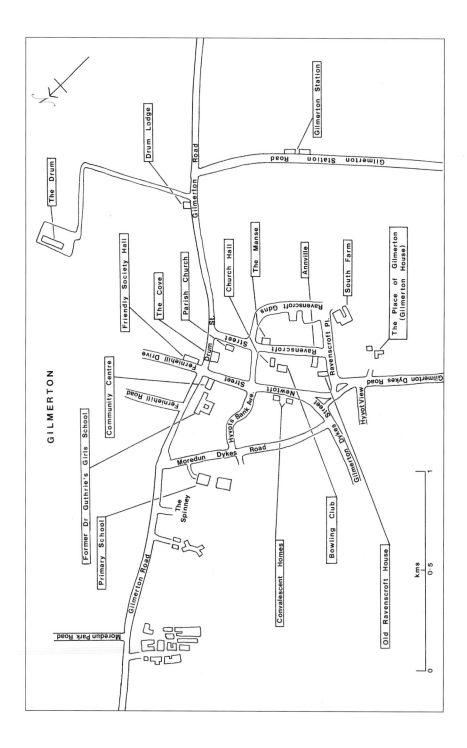

GILMERTON

The Drum

Drum Lodge

Gilmerton Road

Friendly Society Hall

The Cove

Parish Church

Church Hall

The Manse

Annville

South Farm

Ravenscroft Gdns

Ravenscroft

Ravenscroft Pl.

The Place of Gilmerton (Gilmerton House)

Gilmerton Station

Gilmerton Station Road

Community Centre

Former Dr Guthrie's Girls School

Primary School

The Spinney

Ferniehill Road

Ferniehill Drive

Drum St.

Street

Street

Newtoft Street

Hyvots Bank Ave.

Moredun Dykes Road

Gilmerton Dykes Road

HyvotView

Gilmerton Dykes Road

Convalescent Homes

Bowling Club

Old Ravenscroft House

Moredun Park Road

Gilmerton Road

kms

0   0·5   1

CHAPTER TWO

Gilmerton

Gilmerton stands on a ridge of high ground to the south-east of the city, commanding excellent views of Craigmillar Castle, Edinburgh Castle and the Forth estuary. Dating from at least the sixteenth century, Gilmerton's early history was undoubtedly associated with coalmining and limestone quarries, which were worked by successive generations until fairly recent times. A close-knit economy, and insistence on independence from outside sources, meant that much of the working population was engaged in carting coal, lime and sand to various outlets in Edinburgh. Those who were not engaged underground worked on one of the many farms or on the estates of Drum or Gilmerton. Although Gilmerton House and its estate have long since disappeared, that of Drum, to the east of Gilmerton village, is still extant.

Roy's map, dated 1753, shows the layout of the village very similar to its modern form, with the exception of Newtoft Street which was first developed as New Street in the last quarter of the nineteenth century. The village, and its surroundings, may well have developed very differently had a proposal, first made in 1935, come to fruition. In 1934 Edinburgh Town Council acquired seventy-seven acres of ground at Gilmerton, and was in the process of acquiring more land with a view to building a civic airport. The *Edinburgh Evening News* for 25th April 1935 carried a report and a plan of the intended area, immediately south of the Drum estate, and bounded by the roads to Dalkeith and Eskbank. The scheme collapsed under the weight of controversy as a result of which Edinburgh had to wait until 1947 before Turnhouse was extended to include civilian traffic. At the present day, the most obvious development in the village is the emergence of small groups of private housing on land previously used for farming.

A proud day for Euphemia Waldie, crowned Queen at the Gilmerton Children's Gala Day in June 1927. *Courtesy of Miss E. Waldie.*

THE VILLAGE WALK

Gellatly's New Map of the Country 12 Miles Round Edinburgh, dated 1836, describes the area to the west of the village as Gilmerton Place, and names the proprietor of the land as 'Baird Esq.'. It is many years since the Baird family's first connection with the district but as recently as 1989 the same piece of ground was again named Gilmerton Place. This time the setting was a modern housing estate, first planned in the early 1980s by Wimpey Homes, the housebuilders. Prior to the involvement of Wimpey, much of the land lay unused, the previous market garden, owned by the Ritchie family, having been closed many years previously. Robert Ritchie was the last market gardener, whose father, Tom Ritchie, had farmed the land from c. 1900. There was one large house on the site, built in 1951 and extended in 1985, reached from Gilmerton Dykes Road by a long, private driveway from the eastmost of the two original gateways to Gilmerton House. The entrance stonework to this house was redesigned, and the garden ground was reduced in size when the modern houses of Gilmerton Place were built. Although it is an area of great historical importance, well documented by various writers on Edinburgh, very few tangible links with its early history survive. Those that do are worthy of note.

Over the years Mr Baird's estate was variously described as The Place of Gilmerton, Gilmerton Place or Gilmerton House. The mansion lay to the south of the 1951 house and was not fully demolished until the 1970s. Unfortunately, no comprehensive survey was done of Gilmerton House before it was lost completely. One of the few known illustrations appears in *Craigmillar and its Environs*, written by Tom Speedy in 1892. It is shown in heavily wooded policies, as a gabled, pitched-roof structure of probably two storeys with numerous tall chimneys.

The Place of Gilmerton is of great antiquity, dating from at least the middle of the sixteenth century. One of the earliest accounts, in 1792, by the Rev. Thomas Whyte obviously describes the property at the height of its grandeur:

> The mansionhouse has a most excellent site and is favoured with a most charming and delightful prospect on all hands. The like is hardly to be seen anywhere. What is called the long walk on the south side of

the house is peculiarly pleasant. At the east end of it there is a large
arch and above it a balcony in order to enlarge and improve the view.

Grant, in *Old and New Edinburgh*, denotes much of his description to
the early families who owned the property, principally the Kinlochs,
who later built Gilmerton House near Athelstaneford in the 1750s.
George Good, writing in 1893 in *Liberton in Ancient and Modern
Times*, states that the proprietor of the lands of Gilmerton was Sir
David Baird of Newbyth but that the Baird family (in common with
other owners) never occupied the mansion as their home. By the end of
the nineteenth century, Tom Speedy observed that the old house had
been subdivided and tenanted to miners working in the pits near
Gilmerton, and was 'rapidly losing its ancient character'. In 1926 John
Geddie wrote in *The Fringes of Edinburgh* that Gilmerton House
was roofless and nettle-grown and had become an 'abomination of
desolation'.

At the present day the modern housing estate of Gilmerton Place is
the very opposite of Geddie's description, but many of the historical
associations have been lost. The original gate pillars to the mansion
have been repositioned on either side of the new roadway. When the
site was being redeveloped in the early 1980s the old decaying walls
and farm buildings were removed, along with what remained of 'the
Bath'. By then it had been reduced to a small circle of roughly-hewn
stones, about two feet in height, surrounded by the stumps of some
old trees. Originally, the structure was roofed and screened from view
by yew trees planted in the form of a scroll. It is this private aspect
which has given rise to the idea that the building was a bath-house,
probably contemporaneous with the mansion. Much more authentic
detail is available about the ice-house which stood a few hundred yards
to the north of the mansion. In recent years it was examined in great
detail and accurately measured by A. Niven Robertson, who set out
his findings in an article, 'Ice Houses of the Eighteenth and Nineteenth
Centuries' in Volume XXVIII of *The Book of the Old Edinburgh Club*
in 1953. Mr Robertson found that the Gilmerton ice-house was a
vaulted stone chamber forming the basement of a two-storey farm
building situated to the north of the ruined mansion. The construction
was rubble sandstone, roughly eighteen feet from east to west and
fifteen feet from north to south, with walls forty-two inches thick. In

addition to the ice-house, Mr Robertson was able to locate a much larger vaulted chamber, known as 'the dungeon', which may well have formed part of an earlier fortified keep or castle. By the time the site was being cleared for house-building in the 1980s the vault and ice-house had collapsed and were no longer identifiable. Earth-moving equipment did, however, discover an old well which was later filled and capped with concrete.

Two historical features of the Place of Gilmerton have stood the test of time and are still clearly visible, namely the Long Walk and the gazebo referred to by the Rev. Thomas Whyte in 1792. Most of the ground which once formed the Long Walk has been retained as open ground to the south of the new houses. The gazebo, consisting of a large stone arch and balcony, is still in reasonable condition within a private garden reached from the west end of the village.

The original approach to Gilmerton from the west was by Gilmerton Dykes Road, past the Place of Gilmerton, and into the top of Main Street, renamed Ravenscroft Street in 1968. The short cul-de-sac forming the westmost part of Ravenscroft Street is bounded on the north by the red sandstone Westland Cottages built in 1902. The south side offers an intriguing amalgam of dwellings and outhouses surrounded by extensive old walled gardens. The westmost house, Sundial, was built around 1870, probably to replace a much older property, evidence of which can be traced in the boundary walls to the west and north. The garden ground is bounded to the east by the remaining wall of what was probably the dower house of the Place of Gilmerton, and in the garden the original village waterhouse has now been converted into a small dwelling house. The most interesting feature is, however, the early eighteenth-century gazebo platform built over a west-facing arched shelter. From the elevated platform, the remains of the Long Walk are clearly visible beside the modern houses. To the south, the fields of South Farm stretch down to Gilmerton Station Road and the former Gilmerton Station on the Edinburgh, Loanhead and Roslin branch line of the London North Eastern Railway. South Farm, run by the Adams family since 1930, is one of the few working farms still operating within the Edinburgh boundary. In the days when the Brosie Pit was in full production, much of the good-quality coal was transported by rail from the sidings at the pit-head.

We continue eastwards on Ravenscroft Street. On the south side is

Brucefield Place, a row of terraced houses built in 1889, to the east of which are the farm house and steadings of South Farm. On the north side, Annville, a two-storey detached property sitting back from the street, has a slightly projecting centrepiece and a Roman Doric doorway. Occupied formerly as the manse of Gilmerton Parish Church, it is now subdivided into flats and bereft of any garden or foliage to soften its solid lines.

On the same side of the street a short lane runs north to Gilmerton Bowling Club, founded in 1895 with twenty-nine members, most of whom were businessmen and traders in and around the village. In recent years the Club, with the benefit of a greatly increased membership, has extended the premises to include a function hall for over three hundred people. The Club badge depicts a drum, two bowls and a

Baillie William Dow commands the attention of most of the crowd at the unveiling of the First World War Memorial in the grounds of Gilmerton Parish Church.
Courtesy of Miss E. Waldie.

jack, surrounded by a figure-of-eight for the number of players in a rink. Although the badge is intended to symbolise the Drum Estate, in fact the estate takes its name from the word *drum* meaning a hill or ridge.

At about the midway point in Ravenscroft Street several buildings are, or were, used in connection with the school or the church. On the north side is the church hall. It was acquired in 1915 through the generosity of Charles E. Green of Gracemount and greatly extended from its first use as the Montgomery School for Boys and Girls. The large detached house with the stone pilasters on each side of the entrance, and iron finials over the half-dormers, was occupied by Mr Montgomery, the headmaster. Opposite the church hall is the manse, an imposing property with a bargeboard roofline, previously Grahams-ville, the home of one of the village butchers. To the rear of the building, the stable and other out-houses were used in connection with the business. To the east of the manse the small single-storey building with the pantile roof has been used over the years for a variety of church purposes, notably as a workshop for Pioneer Tec.

New housing has been built at Ravenscroft Gardens on the site of Denholm's coal yard and stables. Also on this corner were the Reading Room, latterly equipped with billiard tables, and a small lawn laid out as a putting green. Also on the south side, the village Post Office is housed in a building which was used at different times in the past as a creamery, a private house and a small church. To the rear is the detached red sandstone Limefield House, and adjacent cottage, dating from around 1860. One of the dispositions relating to the house includes reference to Grundie's Well, of which no trace has been found. Opposite the Post Office is a long row of terraced houses, set back from the street with small front gardens and gabled entrances serving adjacent houses.

To the east is Gilmerton Parish Church. The original church, built in 1837, consisted of a shallow-pitched, gabled nave supported by buttresses and topped by a conical-shaped bellcote over the front entrance. This modest building was enlarged in 1882 to include an east and west transept, an entrance porch and a vestry, all designed by John G. Adams. This is substantially the building as it exists today. The opportunity was also taken, in 1882, to renovate the whole interior at a cost of £1,500, of which £500 was contributed by the Baird Trust,

The original Gilmerton Parish Church, built in 1837, was enlarged in 1882 to include an east and west transept, an entrance porch and a vestry, all designed by John G. Adams. *Photograph by Phyllis M. Cant.*

£100 by the Home Mission committee and the remainder by voluntary subscription. On completion, the oak pulpit was gifted by William Ford of Fernieside who was also instrumental in carrying out much of the work of renovation. Although the present building dates from 1837 only, Gilmerton can trace its church history back to the year 1775 when the Rev. John Campbell set up a preaching station and held evening services in the old village. This early pioneering work eventually bore fruit in 1838 when Gilmerton was erected as a Chapel of Ease associated with Liberton Parish Church. The first minister was the Rev. Walter Fairlie, whose allegiance to the Established Church, like that of so many of his contemporaries, was lost to the principles of the Disruption in 1843. In that year he left Gilmerton Parish Church and set up Liberton Free Church in Stenhouse Road (renamed Ellen's Glen Road in 1966 to avoid confusion with the Stenhouse district of Edinburgh, west of Gorgie).

Gilmerton's present minister, the Rev. Donald Skinner, came to the parish in 1962 as his first charge and has remained there ever since. In 1965 he became closely involved in the practical training of youngsters who were leaving school and looking for a worthwhile trade or vocation. From the very earliest days, the idea was to provide them with a useful outlet for their energies and abilities, at the same time introducing them, some for the first time, to the teaching of the Church. The scheme received considerable impetus in 1976 from the introduction of the Government Job Creation Programme, and later the Manpower Services Commission. The Gilmerton scheme operated under the name Pioneer Tec for many years with instruction in engineering and smithcraft, pottery and ceramics, woodwork, knitwear, textiles and tapestries.

At its east end Ravenscroft Street joins Drum Street which is now the main route through the village. As we turn right into Drum Street the long block of houses, with the frontages abutting the pavement, is Innes Buildings, constructed in 1881 by Thomas Innes. The Gardeners' Arms was also built around the same time. Thomas Innes was a builder and horse dealer who lived at Bessieville (probably named after his wife) which stood in its own grounds to the rear of Innes Buildings. The entrance to the house was immediately to the south of the Gardeners' Arms, one solitary gate pier still surviving in the corner of the garage forecourt. A few hundred yards south of the Gardeners' Arms,

The men of the Gilmerton Home Guard – 'Dad's Army' – in 1945. *Courtesy of R. B. Hamilton.*

Gilmerton Play Day in full swing as the band makes its way up Drum Street, south of the junction with Main Street, now Ravenscroft Street. *Courtesy of the late Mary McLean.*

Looking north on Drum Street, towards the junction with New Street, now Newtoft Street. Many of the cottages still exist although some have been converted to commercial use. The entrance to the Cove is on the left behind the horse, and Dr Guthrie's Girls' Industrial School can be seen to the left of the open-topped bus. *Courtesy of A.W. Brotchie.*

on the opposite side of the road, is the West Lodge to the Drum Estate. This is the southern extent of our village walk as the Drum is private property and is not open to the public. Its long and eventful history is, however, recorded in Volume 2 of *Villages of Edinburgh*, published in 1987.

We return to the centre of the village by way of the east pavement. First is the attractive Abbey Lodge Hotel built on the site of some old cottages once used in connection with the Brosie Pit. Adjacent is a row of white-painted terraced houses in which Willie Reilly, tailor and hawker, lived and worked in the 1920s and '30s. His easy payment system of one shilling per week brought comfort and warmth, if not sartorial elegance, within reach of the village population. Opposite Innes Buildings the remaining buildings of East Farm have been renovated and incorporated into new housing. Long gone, however, are the police station and cells which once occupied the north-east corner. Between here and the traffic lights at Newtoft Street is a long line of mainly small buildings, originally constructed as cottages, many of which have since been converted to shops and business premises. Opposite the junction with Ravenscroft Street the two-storey building to the south of the Royal Bank of Scotland has long been known informally as 'the Barracks' or 'the Garrison', believed to have been used at some time in the past by the private army of the Duke of Buccleuch.

The focus of one of Gilmerton's most intriguing stories lies a few yards from the south-west corner of Drum Street and Newtoft Street, yet is surprisingly unknown to many Edinburgh residents. Hacked out of solid stone at a depth of about ten feet below the surface is Gilmerton Cove, one-time dwelling, forge and workshop of the local blacksmith, George Paterson. That Paterson lived and worked in the Cove for many years is beyond doubt, but there is much less agreement over some of the other information recorded by the Rev. Thomas Whyte of Liberton as early as 1792. His account is in *Transactions of the Society of Antiquaries of Scotland:*

> Here is the famous cave dug out of rock by one George Paterson, a smith. It was finished in 1724 after five years hard labour as appears from the inscription on one of the chimney-heads. In this cave are several apartments, several beds, a spacious table with a large punch-bowl all cut out of the rock in the nicest manner. Here there was a forge with a well and washing-house. Here there were several windows which communicated light from above. The author of this extra-ordinary piece of workmanship after he had finished it, lived in it for a long time with his wife and family and prosecuted his business as a smith. He died in it about the year 1735. He was a feuar or feodary and consequently the cave he formed and embellished so much and the garden above it was his own property, and his posterity enjoyed it for some time after his decease. His cave for many years was deemed as a great curiosity and visited by all the people of fashion.

Examination of the Cove reveals a labyrinth of very unusual rooms, passages and tunnels, all cut from the soft sandstone formation. A flight of stone steps leads down to a main passage about forty feet in length

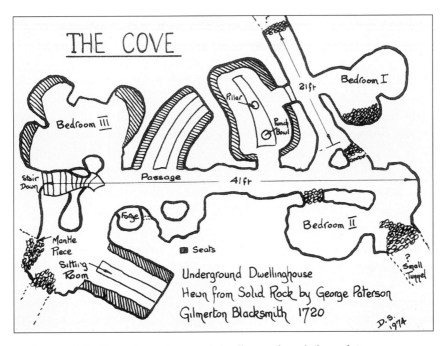

A plan of the Cove, the underground dwelling and workplace of George
Paterson, the local blacksmith. There is considerable controversy over
whether the Cove was hewn out by Paterson himself. *From* Historic
Gilmerton. *Courtesy of the Rev. Donald M. Skinner.*

with rooms off on both sides. To the right-hand side of the passage
there is a forge and a room measuring approximately fourteen feet six
inches by seven feet, with headroom of about six feet. At one end of
this room there is a stone mantlepiece and at the other end a stone
table seven feet long with benches on each side. The arrangement of
rooms on the left-hand side of the main passage is more elaborate. The
first room is tucked in behind the staircase, and the next, measuring
only eight feet by five feet, has all the available floor space taken up
with a narrow stone table and benches on each side. The third room,
on the left, is the famous drinking parlour, fifteen feet long with a
ten-foot long table into which has been hollowed a stone basin. The
ceiling in this room is supported by a roughly cut pillar. The parlour
leads into a subsidiary passage running at approximately right angles
to the main passage, and beyond the subsidiary passage there is another
room. At its furthest point from the entrance steps, the main passage
curves slightly to the right into the last room, from which there appears

to be the start of a tunnel. There is no definite evidence as to the purpose of the tunnel, but there has been no shortage of ingenious suggestions, including an escape route from Craigmillar Castle some two miles to the north-east.

The existence of the Cove has been well documented in various publications since the account in 1792 by the Rev. Thomas Whyte, but, generally, these have merely repeated what Whyte says. In November 1897 a much more scientific approach was adopted by F. R. Coles, Assistant Keeper of the National Museum of Antiquities of Scotland, who visited the Cove in the company of J. Balfour Paul and George Good F.S.A. Their findings were set out in the *Proceedings of the Society of Antiquaries of Scotland*, and represent a major challenge to the theory that the Cove was constructed by George Paterson. According to Coles, the Cove could not have been hewn out in five years by one man, and the nature of the tool-work on the stone suggested a date much earlier than the eighteenth century. Indeed all Coles' evidence suggests that Paterson merely used the Cove in the mid-eighteenth century, but was not its architect. Many questions remain unanswered, the most pertinent of which is whether Paterson is buried in the Cove,

The famous drinking parlour in the Cove, photographed in 1987. The curved stone table has a hollowed-out punch bowl and a column of stone supporting the roof. *Photograph by Graham C. Cant.*

as suggested by the words of the early eighteenth-century poet Alexander Pennycuik:

> Upon the earth thrives villainy and woe,
> But happiness and I do dwell below,
> My hands hewed out this rock into a cell,
> Wherein from din of life I safely dwell.
> On Jacob's pillow nightly lies my head,
> My house when living and my grave when dead.
> Inscribe upon it, when I'm dead and gone,
> I lived and died within my mother's womb.

Coles was never able to confirm any trace of the above inscription which was said to be cut into the stonework above the fireplace. Clearly the Cove has not yet given up all its secrets. At the present day it is not accessible to the public but there are moves afoot to make it so.

Within a short distance of the junction of Drum Street, Newtoft Street, Gilmerton Road and Ferniehill Drive there are several buildings which have been used for a variety of educational and recreational purposes over the years.

On the south-east corner the small single-storey building, with the pitched roof, is the former Hall of the Junior Friendly Society. Above the front door is a stone plaque with the words: JUNIOR FRIENDLY SOCIETY 1787 – HALL BUILT 1888. The Society was constituted 'for the purpose of relieving such of its Members who by sickness or lameness should occasionally be rendered unable to attend their usual employment, and for defraying the funeral expenses of such of them or their Wives, at death'. Although the Society no longer exists, several documents and books of account were deposited some years ago with the Edinburgh Room of Edinburgh Central Library. One of the earliest entries, dated 21st December 1808, under the heading 'Widows Annuities', records regular payments of 15/- (75p) to Widow Anderson, Widow Hoggarth and other deserving cases. Anyone admitted to the Society had to be of good moral character, between twelve and thirty years of age, and free from all constitutional and hereditary disease. Entry money, payable each quarter, was on an age-related scale. The penalty for cheating was instant dismissal from the Society, and all benefit was lost:

If any member feign himself sick or lame or be convicted of bringing trouble on himself by any immoral behaviour or vicious and irregular conduct and refuse the instruction of a Physician he shall lose all right; and if his trouble should appear to be the venereal disorder; or the result of it; or to proceed from any excessive drinking; or from fighting; or any other irregularity he shall exclude himself from the Society.

For many years the Gilmerton Play Day was closely associated with the activities of the Junior Friendly Society. Had the Rev. James Begg of Liberton Church taken the Laird of Moredun's advice to 'draw the manse blinds' on this great annual event, the *New Statistical Account of Scotland* would have been robbed of one of its most interesting accounts of Gilmerton life in the 1840s, as observed through the manse window:

> The only peculiar games here are what are called 'carters' plays'. The carters have friendly societies for the purpose of supporting each other in old age or during ill-health and with a view partly of securing a day's recreation, and partly of recruiting their numbers and funds, they have an annual procession. Every man decorates his cart-horse with flowers and ribbons and a regular procession is made accompanied by a band of music through this and some of the neighbouring parishes. To crown all, there is an uncouth uproarious race with cart-horses on the public road, which draws forth a crowd of Edinburgh idlers and all ends in a dinner for which a fixed sum is paid. Much rioting and profligacy often take place in connection with these amusements and the whole scene is melancholy. There are other societies in the parish which have also annual parades with a similar result. These societies have undoubtedly been in some respects useful but the 'plays' are fortunately rapidly declining; and it is to be hoped that savings banks in which there is neither risk nor temptation to drunkenness will soon become the universal depositories for the surplus earnings of the people.

Despite the Rev. James Begg's wish that the Play Days be restricted, they existed for another hundred years without the need for rioting, profligacy and drunkenness, but were in serious decline in the years prior to the Second World War, and never returned to their former glory. The former Hall of the Society in Drum Street is currently used by Fernieside Boys' Club.

Gilmerton Community Centre was built as Gilmerton Public School in 1914 to replace the much smaller Anderson Female School on the same site. *Photograph by Phyllis M. Cant.*

Diagonally opposite the Society Hall is a much grander building used, since 1984, as Gilmerton Community Centre. It was designed by J. Inch Morrison and opened as a school on 11th September 1914 by Lady Susan Gilmour, wife of the Chairman of the School Board. In deference to the original founders of the Anderson Female School (which had previously stood on the site) the new school laboured under the rather awkward name of Gilmerton, The Anderson Public School until 1926 when it was renamed Gilmerton Public School. The present janitor's house is all that remains of the original Anderson Female School building. Prior to the opening of the Gilmerton Anderson school, pupils were taught at Liberton Free Church School in Ellen's Glen Road between 1843 and 1874, and thereafter at the Green Halls in Main Street, now Ravenscroft Street.

To the north of Gilmerton Community Centre is the former Dr Guthrie's Girls' School building, harled and with red sandstone dressings, designed by McArthy & Watson in 1903. The front entrance has a steeply pedimented overdoor with the name in gold – DR GUTHRIE'S GIRLS' INDUSTRIAL SCHOOL 1904 – and above, the initials I.S.B. for Industrial School Board.

Dr Thomas Guthrie, preacher, philanthropist and writer, was born in Brechin on 12th July 1803, and died at St Leonards, Hastings on 24th February 1873, a fraction short of his allotted three score and ten years. His energetic lifestyle, however, produced a catalogue of achievement which by normal standards would have taken much longer than

The pedimented portals of Dr Guthrie's Girls' Industrial School, designed by McArthy & Watson in 1903, was opened in 1904 and closed in 1986. It is now the headquarters of the Faith Mission and Bible College. *Photograph by Phyllis M. Cant.*

Dr Thomas Guthrie, preacher, philanthropist and writer, pioneered the success of the Ragged Schools on the simple philosophy of Patience, Prayer and Porridge. *From Disruption Worthies, 1876.*

a lifetime. Born of parents already established in Christian beliefs, Thomas studied at Edinburgh University from 1815 and was licensed to preach in 1825. His first charge was at Arbirlot near Arbroath in 1830, after spending the intervening period studying science and medicine at Edinburgh and Paris. When news of his transfer, in 1837, to Old Greyfriars in Edinburgh, reached his parishioners at Arbirlot, it is said that 'they were a' greetin'', knowing full well that they were losing a man who would be almost impossible to replace. On his arrival in Edinburgh he spent three years at Old Greyfriars and then entered the new church of St John's, formed from the Old Greyfriars parish. Having already spent many years campaigning against Patronage in the church, it was no surprise to see him among the leaders of the Disruption with Dr Chalmers in 1843. Not only was he committed to its principles but he led a massive campaign immediately thereafter and raised £116,000 under the Manse Scheme for homeless ministers.

In Edinburgh, however, Dr Guthrie will always be remembered primarily for his creation of, and dedication to, the Original Ragged Schools. His philosophy was simple, easily understood and uncomfortably difficult to ignore: Patience, Prayer and Porridge; porridge first and the other two might follow. In 1847 Guthrie acquired rooms in Ramsay Lane in Castlehill where he took in seven boys, and later thirteen girls, who would otherwise have received no education and little guidance. By the end of the first year he was providing food, clothing and education for almost four hundred and fifty children. The pattern was set. The Ragged School concept spread throughout Scotland and was given further impetus by the Education Act of 1872 which provided Government grants to augment money raised by public subscription. After his death, a school for boys was opened at Liberton in 1888 and for girls at Gilmerton in 1904. In 1932 the system of Approved Schools was implemented and replaced in 1969 by List D Schools in liaison with Children's Panels. In the mid-1980s the Girls' school at Gilmerton closed its doors for the last time, the remaining pupils being transferred to Wellington School near Penicuik.

Dr Thomas Guthrie is buried in Grange Cemetery. In West Princes Street Gardens, opposite the junction of Princes Street and Castle Street, there is an imposing statue of this early Victorian philanthropist. The

The new Bible College and Headquarters of the Faith Mission were officially opened on Saturday 23rd May 1987, attended by 1,300 guests.
From The New Faith Mission and Bible College. *Photograph by the Rev. Dr. Colin N. Peckham.*

huge fatherly figure of Guthrie, skilfully cut by F. W. Pomeroy in 1911, towers above the much slighter figure of a wee lad from the Ragged School, yet to be enriched by the philosophy of the day – Patience, Prayer and Porridge.

Dr Guthrie's school building at Gilmerton lay empty for some time before being acquired, in 1986, by the Faith Mission who were then operating from two buildings in the Ravelston area, and another at Coates Gardens. The Faith Mission was founded by John George Govan of Glasgow, in 1886, 'as an interdenominational society for the evangelization of the rural areas of Great Britain'. It operates throughout Scotland, Northern Ireland, the Republic of Ireland and in parts of England, each being divided into districts, controlled by separate district headquarters. By 1890 John Govan felt the need for a training centre for his workers, first established at Rothesay and then transferred to Joppa in 1912. In the following year, the Mission received a substantial gift of money from Lord MacLay, a wealthy shipowner, which enabled it to buy a house for training young workers at Ravelston Park in Edinburgh. This was followed in 1932 by a further gift, from the same source, which financed the purchase of a nearby property at No. 1 Ravelston Dykes. These two properties, with the addition of the headquarters at No. 38 Coates Gardens, accommmodated the work of the Mission for several decades until the transfer to Gilmerton in 1986 – which happened to be the centenary year. Although the proceeds of the sale of the existing properties were sufficient to finance the purchase of the Gilmerton building, a huge amount of work was still needed to bring the new premises up to the standard required for the New Bible College and headquarters of the Faith Mission. The combined efforts of many enthusiastic volunteers from the Mission, and a few key professionals, completely transformed the building: the old sewing room and the punishment room became accommodation for staff and married students; the domestic science room became the kitchen; and the gymnasium became the dining room. Main services to the building were renewed and the interior was redecorated and furnished in time for the official opening on Saturday 23rd May 1987.

At the present day, the building is home to the Faith Mission Headquarters and the Bible College which attracts many students annually. In addition there are facilities for hosting the annual Edinburgh Convention which attracts up to 500 delegates. The history of

Robbie Pentland has lived in the village of Gilmerton all his life. He is photographed here in 1998 outside his cottage in Newtoft Street, formerly New Street. The cottages were built for £50 each in the 1870s by Thomas Innes of Gilmerton.

Dr Peacock in his well-sprung carriage at Stenhouse, near Gilmerton, *c.* 1890.

the organisation, *The New Faith Mission Bible College*, by the Rev. Dr Colin N. Peckham, Principal of the College, was published in 1994.

At the end of the nineteenth century New Street (now Newtoft Street) was a very minor road with only a few buildings on the north and south sides. Innes Cottages at the south-west end were extended from a single cottage which stood on its own for many years surrounded by fields of corn. The principal buildings on the north side were first occupied as Convalescent Homes. The first home (eastmost building) was Ravenscroft, established in 1878 with the object of providing 'convalescent treatment for men and women of the working class whose means are exhausted owing to illness'. Admission for a stay of two or three weeks was free, but applicants had to be respectable, necessitous, free from infectious disease, and recommended by a clergyman or respectable householder known to one of the trustees. In 1889 the Home held a Grand Musical Conversazione in the Balfour Banquet Hall, Waverley Market on Friday 6th December with entertainment under the personal direction of H. H. Morell Mackenzie of London. The programme included several *tableaux vivants* depicting the lives of Queen Mary, John Knox and Prince Charles Edward Stuart, interspersed with music by the Band of the Grenadier Guards. The proceeds provided greatly needed funds for the upkeep of the Adults' Home as well as the Children's Convalescent Home first established in 1881. Children, admitted at the rate of about two hundred and fifty each year, were referred from the Sick Children's Hospital, the Royal Infirmary and Leith Hospital. A new children's home was opened by the Very Rev. Dean Montgomery on 18th December 1888 to accommodate twenty-two patients, including one special unit for a mother and child. Generally speaking, the children were from poor families but were admitted free under various charitable trusts. A plaque on the west wall of the westmost building bears the entwined initials C.C.H. (Children's Convalescent Home) in the centre with the date 1888. At the present day the eastmost building is occupied as residential flats and the westmost building is unoccupied.

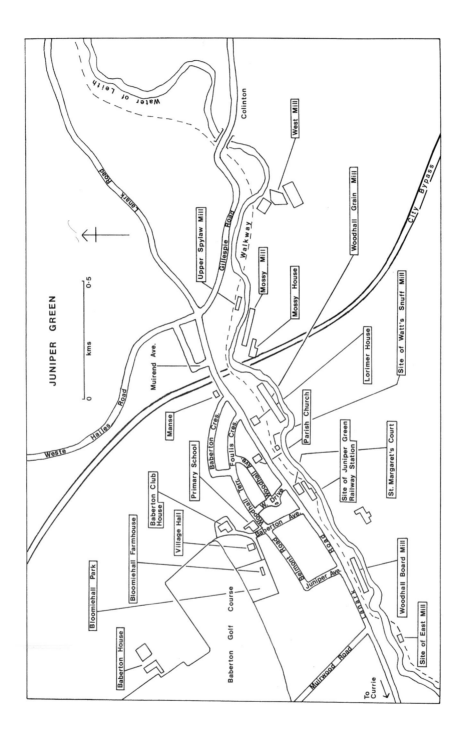

JUNIPER GREEN

kms

0   0·5

Water of Leith

Colinton

West Mill

Woodhall Grain Mill

City Bypass

Lanark Road

Upper Spylaw Mill

Gillespie Road

Walkway

Mossy Mill

Mossy House

Site of Watt's Snuff Mill

Lorimer House

Muirend Ave.

Weste   Halles   Road

Manse

Baberton Cres.

Foulis Cres.

Parish Church

Site of Juniper Green Railway Station

St. Margaret's Court

Primary School

Telford Ave.

Thompson Ave.

Baberton Club House

Village Hall

W. Drive

Bloomiehall Farmhouse

Baberton Ave.

Baberton Road

Bloomiehall Park

Baberton House

Baberton Golf Course

Belmont Road

Juniper Ave.

Woodhall Board Mill

Muirwood Road

Lanark Road

Site of East Mill

To Currie

CHAPTER THREE

Juniper Green

Juniper Green, lying between Colinton and Currie, developed around the numerous industries powered by the Water of Leith. The village formed a natural hinterland for the thriving mills which were frequently built in very restricted positions as near as possible to the best source of water power. Although it is known that mills were operating along the valley from at least the sixteenth century, Juniper Green did not develop as a distinct community until very much later. *Adair's Map* of 1735 shows the line of what is now Lanark Road passing through Curriemoor, but the only places of habitation shown are Baberton to the north and Woodhall to the south. The position had not altered much by 1766 when *Laurie* drew up his map showing Baberton, Fairniflat, W. Hales (sic) and Curriemuirend. It was not until well into the nineteenth century that the village took on anything like its present-day layout. There was a sufficiently large population in 1843 to support the newly formed Free Church, and in 1874 Juniper Green railway station was opened by the Caledonian Railway Company. The railway greatly improved communications for passengers and freight. Increased prosperity saw the construction of large detached houses along both sides of Lanark Road, many by eminent architects of the day. After Edinburgh was extended in 1920 to include Juniper Green, extensive bungalow development took place on the north side of the village.

The origin of the name 'Juniper Green' is uncertain although tradition has it that the name is taken from the juniper bush which is said to have been prevalent in the district. However, according to *The Place Names of Edinburgh* by Stuart Harris, at least one authority has questioned this theory, namely the Rev. John Walker, who stated in *Walker's Collington*, 1795, that he had been unable to find any juniper plants growing in the district at that time. Whatever the origin is, the name is certainly unique. During the Second World War, when the troopship *The Empress of Canada* reached Cape Town, Dr Ross, serving with the Royal Army Medical Corps, sent a cable to his wife, who lived at Juniper Green. The postmaster at Cape Town was intrigued by the name 'Juniper Green', but, after consulting his World Gazetteer, announced that there was only one such place in the world, and that it was a recognised postal address. Any cable addressed simply 'Juniper Green' would eventually arrive, although he could not guarantee when!

Masons, with caps, pipes, and aprons, employed on building villas at Curriemuirend *c*. 1902.

THE VILLAGE WALK

At the east end of Juniper Green the elegant detached houses near Gillespie Crossroads were constructed around 1900, but traditionally the old village does not start until Curriemuirend. The name is commemorated in Muirend Avenue on the north side of Lanark Road, opposite Tanners, previously the Pentland Arms. To the west of Tanners, beside modern flatted property, the remaining frontage of an old two-storey house marks the approximate position of the road which gave access to the mills before the construction of the City Bypass. The village landscape was completely altered at this point by the line of the new road round the south of Edinburgh. This required the re-siting of Juniper Green Bowling Green which had been on the north side of Lanark Road, and the shoring up of the garden ground around the manse belonging to Juniper Green Parish Church. The ground on the south-west side of the Bypass, formerly occupied by Woodhall Nurseries, has been partly redeveloped for modern housing in contrast to the two older properties to the west. The first of these is Southernwood from which Dr John M. Ross M.B.E. ran his practice for many years. The second was originally named Torduff, a large detached house of white harl and red tiles, in wooded grounds, built in 1905 to designs by Robert S. Lorimer for a Miss Bruce. It is now used as a nursing home, taking the name Lorimer House after its architect.

Between Foulis Crescent and Woodhall Drive, the handsome Gothic lines of Juniper Green Parish Church share the north side with a variety of individually designed villas, one of which, Castle Bank, has a most interesting castellated frontage, built in 1845 for its first owner, James Fortune. On the south side of the road several houses, built much later, have retained their original names: Pentland View, Broughton and many others.

Although Juniper Green's churches cannot claim great antiquity, nevertheless the circumstances in which the first congregations were established are interesting in relation to the religious thinking of the day. Prior to 1843 the inhabitants of Juniper Green travelled to either Colinton or Currie for Sunday worship. At the famous Disruption in 1843, however, neither the minister at Colinton nor the minister at Currie 'came out' in support of Dr Chalmers and his supporters. It followed, therefore, that although Free Churches were springing up all

491/42 U.F. Church, Juniper Green

Juniper Green Parish Church was built as a Free Church in 1879 to replace the much smaller Colinton and Currie Free Church established on the same site in 1844.

A group of all ages from the congregation of St Margaret's Parish Church which stood on the south side of Lanark Road from 1897 to c.1979 when it was demolished. Unfortunately, the date of the photograph and details of the event have not been established. *Courtesy of Gordon Renwick*.

over Edinburgh and throughout Scotland, there was no focal point for Disruptionists in the area from Colinton to Currie. This was remedied by protesters holding services in Society Hall at Currie and the Old Ballroom in Colinton. In 1844 the Rev. Harry Anderson was ordained as minister of Currie and Colinton Free Church, and, in the following year, a feu charter was obtained from Sir William Liston Foulis, Bart., for a piece of land 'on the North side of the Turnpike Road leading from Edinburgh to Lanark', on which to build a permanent church. The Rev. Harry Anderson was succeeded by the Rev. Charles McNeil in 1870. During the following decade it became clear that the fairly modest church erected in 1845 was insufficient for the congregation's needs, and in 1879 James Fairley, the architect, was employed to draw up plans for a much bigger church. The resulting building, still in use today, was erected in a raised position, with a central bellcote above the front entrance on the south-facing gable, flanked by pairs of twin towers at different heights. Before this imposing structure was con- secrated, it played host to one of the greatest orators of the day – Mr Gladstone – during the famous Midlothian Campaign of 1879–1880. On completion, the church was named Juniper Green Free Church, and was renamed St Andrew's Juniper Green in 1929.

Whilst Juniper Green had a Free Church almost from the time of the Disruption in 1843, it was not until about 1890 that members of the Church of Scotland in Juniper Green were successful in their bid to establish a local church. An iron church, previously in use at Craiglockhart, was purchased and erected on the north side of Lanark Road a few yards west of the junction with Woodhall Drive. As soon as sufficient funds were available, a site, previously occupied by a dairy on the south side of Lanark Road, was obtained for the erection of a stone church. Drawings were prepared by the architect R. M. Cameron and the foundation stone was laid in 1895 for a red sandstone Gothic church by the local builders, Messrs Turner of Juniper Green. The new church, named St Margaret's, was opened on 23rd January 1897.

In 1974 the congregations of St Andrew's and St Margaret's were united under the new name Juniper Green Parish Church. St Andrew's Church was retained for worship and the St Margaret's building was demolished and replaced by a block of flats in 1979. The flats, approp- riately named St Margaret's Court, were built on the site of the main church, the only part retained being a stone cross from the roof which is incorporated as a feature near the entrance doorway. The stone-built hall, erected in 1913, has also been saved and forms the function hall of St Margaret's Court.

In the vestibule of Juniper Green Parish Church there are three plaques facing the front entrance: the central copper plaque was brought from St Margaret's and confirms the date of dedication on 23rd January 1897; to the left there is a War Memorial, also brought from St Margaret's, commemorating those of the parish who fell in the First World War; and to the right is the War Memorial of the former St Andrew's Church commemorating those who fell in both World Wars.

Immediately west of St Margaret's Court lies the heart of the old village bounded by Baberton Avenue, Belmont Road, Juniper Avenue (formerly Belmont Avenue) and Lanark Road. Juniper Green School has been located in Baberton Avenue for a very long time, albeit in a variety of buildings. Halfway along on the east side, the building with the long windows, previously occupied by the school janitor, was once the Female Subscription School. A new building was erected on the site of the Free Church School at the junction of Baberton Avenue and Woodhall Terrace, and in more recent times another building has been

Southernwood, on the south side of Lanark Road, from which Dr John M. Ross, M.B.E. ran his practice for many years.

A moment's respite for the members of the 'World's Famous Blue Hungry Band' in Baberton Avenue outside Juniper Green Primary School. *Courtesy of Gordon Renwick.*

erected on the open ground to the north, near the clubhouse of Baberton Golf Club. One of the best known of the early headmasters was Peter Malloch who taught at Juniper Green from 1876 to 1899 and took a keen interest in the history of the village. Although he never published a formal history of the district, his copious notes have been of great value to subsequent researchers. So great was the respect for Mr Malloch that in 1955, many years after his death, a group of about seventy ex-pupils met at the old school to pay their respects to their late headmaster. Among those who attended were 94-year-old Tom Napier, Sir David Henry of Auckland, and Andrew B. Dea, Rector of Bo'ness Academy.

At the north end of Baberton Avenue a long tree-lined, private road leads to Baberton House, lying in extensive wooded policies and flanked on two sides by Baberton Golf Course. Well into the twentieth century this entrance was marked by high railings and gates adjoining a lodge house on the east side of the driveway. Baberton House, previously known as Kilbaberton, dates from at least 1622, although the vaulted ground-floor rooms may be of earlier date. It was built for James Murray, Master of the King's Works, on land granted to him by James VI. The 1622 double-L plan of three storeys created a south-facing courtyard with stair turrets built into the two angles. The basic structure was harled rubble, greatly enhanced by many fine architectural features incorporated on the windows, door and chimneys. The most significant alteration to the house was in 1765 when the courtyard was filled in by a semi-octagonal bay projecting to the south.

The 1765 bay appears on a map of uncertain date produced in the course of a legal dispute over a small area of ground on the south side of the estate. As the map bears the title 'Baberton Plans taken from the plan drawn by Mr Mather in 1755', it seems likely that the information needed for the legal dispute has merely been superimposed on Mr Mather's map of 1755. Nevertheless, the topographical information is interesting. No trees are shown on the north or south driveway, although numerous trees are shown forming the boundary with Mr Carmichael's ground to the east. On the west side of the estate, going north is 'Road to Hermiston on the Glasgow Road', and, going south, 'Road to Currie on the Sclatefoord Road'. On the east side of the estate is a road following approximately the line of the old Wester Hailes Road past Fernieflat. The long narrow piece of land in dispute, wedged between the east boundary of Baberton and the west boundary of Mr Carmichael's land, is rather quaintly described as 'Gushet in Dispute'. Unfortunately, no record of the final outcome of the dispute has been traced.

In 1847 a further survey of the Baberton estate was undertaken by George Buchanan, Civil Engineer. He was employed by the Caledonian Railway Company to draw plans and sections for proposed alterations to the 'Parish Road and Approach to Baberton House' created by the coming of the railway. The Parish Road ran straight from north-east to south-west, and the proposed railway line was also to run in the same direction but nearer to an east-west axis. To facilitate the cross-over, the roadway was excavated to a depth where it could turn under the new railway bridge in an awkward S-bend. On completion, the railway bisected the Baberton estate, separating the farm buildings of Baberton Mains on the north side of the Parish Road from Baberton House on the south side.

To this day the awkward S-bend must be negotiated in approaching Baberton House from the north. The north entrance leads up a tarmac drive to imposing double gates set into a walled courtyard. Baberton House, the headquarters of Cruden Investments Ltd. since 1980, is maintained in excellent condition in well-tended policies of several acres. Despite its three centuries of use, many of the original features can clearly be seen. On the south-facing wall of the original house, a window pediment on the east flank bears the date 1622 and the initials

Baberton House, previously known as Kilbaberton, was built in the early seventeenth century for James Murray, Master of the King's Works. It is now the headquarters of Cruden Investments Ltd.
Courtesy of M. R. A. Matthews.

I.M. for James Murray. A similar window on the west flank bears the initials K.W. for Katherine Weir, wife of James Murray. The north façade contains three interesting half-dormer windows: the centre one has the date 1623; the eastmost bears the initials I.M; and the westmost appears to be blank. The elegant semi-octagonal bay to the south contains some of the principal rooms of the house, dating from 1765. The date appears above the doorway and below an octagonal-shaped crest, divided diagonally by a serrated cross with a five-point star in each segment.

At the close of the nineteenth century Baberton estate was owned by Sir James Gibson Craig, Bart., who leased part of the land in 1893 for the construction of Baberton Golf Course. The original nine-hole course, designed by Willie Park, was opened on 15th July 1893, but within a very short time it was extended to eighteen holes. Membership was initially restricted to residents of the parishes of Colinton and Currie, but, when the course was extended, the opportunity was taken to admit a limited number of non-resident members. The non-resident membership rapidly increased to three hundred, far outnumbering the local membership which remained fairly constant at around one hundred. In recognition of their increased numbers, non-resident members were given representation on the Committee. Baberton can claim to be the birthplace of the steel-shafted golf club, a patent application having been taken out on 1st May 1894 by Thomas Horsburgh who was later captain of the club from 1914 to 1917 and again from 1929 to 1931.

The first clubhouse, designed in 1896 by the architect David McArthy, was replaced in 1902 by a much grander building designed by J. N. Scott and A. Lorne Campbell. This building has subsequently been extended on numerous occasions over the years. The Jubilee celebrations, scheduled to take place in 1943, were postponed until 8th June 1946 when plaques were unveiled in memory of the members who had fallen in the Second World War, and to commemorate the Jubilee. Shortly after the Jubilee the club suffered severely from an extensive fire on 22nd March 1948 which destroyed the dining room and the ladies' room.

In the post-war years Baberton has steadily built up its membership and has improved the playing surface out of all recognition from the first nine-hole course, hemmed in by menacing rough and formidable

RTON GOLF HOUSE

Baberton Golf Clubhouse was designed in 1902 by J. M. Scott and A. Lorne Campbell and has been extended on several occassions since. *From* Views of Juniper Green and District.

hazards. At a height of four hundred feet above sea level, and commanding extensive views over the city and the Forth, Baberton Golf Club maintains great sporting traditions, albeit somewhat more refined than in the days when Baberton was used as a hunting estate by James VI and his entourage.

In 1993 the club produced a centenary history, *Baberton Golf Club: the First Hundred Years*, which reviews in a thorough, but lighthearted style, the formation and growth of the club since inception. The Men's Amateur par is 69 and the course record is 64, currently held equally by R. W. Bradly in 1989, D. Beveridge Jnr., in 1991 and B. J. H. Tait in 1992. The Ladies' Amateur record for the par 72 course is 67, set in 1997 by Karen Marshall which replaced the previous record of 68 held since 1982 by her mother Joan Marshall. The professional course record is 62 recorded by Brian Barnes in 1981.

At the top of Baberton Avenue, to the west of the entrance to Baberton Golf Club, is the village hall, now used as a Community Centre with much the same aims as when it was first built. The hall was started in 1900 by the local Company of Volunteers but in 1910, when the Volunteers were disbanded, the hall was purchased on behalf

Led by the local 'bobby', almost the entire population of the old village appears to have turned out for the Juniper Green Co-operative Society Children's Gala Day, instituted in 1901.

Watched by a smaller crowd, and with fewer followers, is the band leading the 4/5th Royal Scots Volunteers *c.* 1900, in Baberton Avenue.

Dressed for the occasion, to show off their very latest delivery van, is the
staff of the Juniper Green Co-operative Society Ltd.

of Trustees. For many years the organisation was undertaken by
the Young Men's Club but membership dwindled and by 1957 the
building was in need of substantial repairs. Juniper Green Village
Association was formed to represent all the interests in the district, and
funds were raised to put the hall and the caretaker's house in good
order. The constitution of the Association, drawn up on 9th July 1957
under the chairmanship of Alec Wallace, laid out the main aims and
objects.

To the west of the village hall one of the oldest buildings in Juniper
Green stands close to the entrance to Bloomiehall Public Park. This
long single-storey building was constructed originally as byres for
Bloomiehall Farm, but is now a private house. Adjacent is Bloomiehall
Farmhouse, a neat two-storey house with unusual castellated stonework
on its east side. Prior to 1974 it was used by the park keeper at
Bloomiehall Park but when he retired there was local anxiety that the
house might be demolished. Fortunately, it was bricked up and protected against vandalism until 1978 when it was put up for sale as a
private residence. The *Evening News* report of 11th March 1978 pro-
claimed the house 'For Sale – this former Royal residence' – a reference

The proprietors outside a typical village 'sweetie' shop in Belmont Avenue, now Juniper Avenue. The shop obviously carried a good stock of 'Victory V Gums' and 'Victory Chlorodyne Lozs', among other favourites. *Courtesy of Gordon Renwick.*

to the belief that Bonnie Prince Charlie had slept there on his way to Edinburgh with his troops before the Battle of Prestonpans in 1745.

The last section of Lanark Road, west of Baberton Avenue, has several houses of historic interest. At No. 547 the large L-plan dwelling on the south side was formerly the manse for St Margaret's Church and, before that, was the Dower House to Woodhall in the eighteenth century. Further west, at the city boundary, the neat cottage beside the former Veitch's Garden Centre takes the name Enterkin from Enterkins Yett, the north entrance to Woodhall House.

THE MILLS BY THE WATER OF LEITH

The mills on the Juniper Green section of the Water of Leith are more than a century older than the village, and must, therefore, be regarded as the original focus of population between Colinton and Currie.

Although it is still possible to locate the site of many of these mills, the topography of the area has greatly altered from the days when grain, flax, paper and snuff were produced. From at least the sixteenth century, mills were located on the north and south banks at strategic points where a weir and lade could be built to give the maximum head of water to power the machinery. The pathway, or rudimentary road-way, linking these small settlements alternated between the north and south banks according to the spread of population, and the existence of fords where people and carts could cross. Access to the turnpike roads of the neighbourhood was generally up the steep embankment on the north side of the Water of Leith.

In the late 1860s the Caledonian Railway Company surveyed the Water of Leith valley with a view to laying a spur, from the main track at Slateford, to Balerno. Authority to build the railway was obtained on 20th June 1870 and the line was opened to traffic on 1st August 1874 with stations at Colinton, Juniper Green and Currie. The steep-sided valley dictated that only a single track was laid, requiring several bridges and cuttings, as well as realignment of access roads, and the provision of level-crossing gates. Passenger services ceased on 30th October 1943 but goods trains used the line until the 1960s. Thereafter the track lay derelict for several years before being renovated as a public walkway. From this walkway it is possible, with patience and imagin-ation, to reconstruct some of the flavour of the locality in the days when Juniper Green's economy was firmly based on water-powered mills.

One of the most convenient access points to the Juniper Green section of the walkway is near the former West Mill, at the foot of West Mill Road, Colinton. Adjacent to the site of the former Bonaly Dairy, the walkway crosses over the original mill lade which can be seen running eastwards (downstream) towards the old mill complex. To the west, the lade is lined in concrete for a short distance and, although not in use, appears to be capable of holding water, especially after periods of heavy rainfall. The present buildings at West Mill are of modern appearance, but grain and flour mills, and waulk mills where cloth was beaten or thrashed, operated here from at least the late seventeenth century. In the eighteenth and nineteenth centuries the main products were grain and paper, and well within living memory the mill was used for the manufacture of Cerebos Salt and Scott's Porage Oats.

The walkway proceeds westwards from West Mill on what was a long straight section of single-track railway. The Water of Leith lies on the right at a much lower level, and on the left, the mill lade runs for several hundred yards between the walkway and the long gardens at the back of the former mill cottages. As the path begins to curve to the left, the first bridge is immediately ahead, crossing to the opposite bank of the Water of Leith. The single-arch stone bridge was designed to carry the railway and is, therefore, of much stronger construction than is required for pedestrian use only. From its left-hand parapet the weir (or waterfall) for the former West Mill can be seen with the entrance sluice at the head of the lade.

To the west of the bridge at the West Mill weir a paddock and range of stables on the left form part of the policies of Upper Spylaw Mill. This is one of the oldest and best-preserved mill buildings in the valley, the main entrance to which was protected by the original level-crossing gate. The narrow road up the steep slope on the right provides vehicular

Seventeenth-century Upper Spylaw Mill, 1986, in the valley of the Water of Leith with the walkway on the left constructed on the old railway line to Balerno. *Photograph by Graham C. Cant.*

access from Gillespie Road. Upper Spylaw Mill is believed to date from 1681 when it formed an integral part of the papermaking industry in the valley. A century later it was producing snuff along with several other mills at Colinton and Juniper Green. Its transformation to a dairy around 1880 is recorded in the colourful language of John Geddie in 1898 when he says in *The Home Country of Robert Louis Stevenson*: 'The Water wheel sulks in its dark chamber; but there are cream barrels and butter-milk pails where brown Taddy was ground for the noses of our great-grandfathers'. These cream barrels and milk pails were the everyday tools of trade of the Trail family who ran the dairy and piggery from 1880 to 1930, after which Upper Spylaw Mill was used as a riding school. In 1960, however, third-generation descendants of the Trails re-established the family connection when Mr and Mrs Downie purchased the mill as a private dwelling. Fortunately, the Downies resisted professional advice to demolish the mill, preferring instead to undertake an extensive programme of repair and renovation. This imaginative stand against the general trend of the 1960s has conserved the exterior stonework, almost intact, and much of the interior. Unfortunately nothing remains of the mill machinery although it is possible to detect the position of the lade and the point on the west wall at which it entered the mill to drive the wheel and machinery.

Immediately west of Upper Spylaw Mill the dilapidated buildings of the former Mossy Mill can be seen through the trees on the south bank. Several small businesses occupied this extensive brick-built complex but there is very little mill atmosphere now. The high square chimneys have long since gone and there is little evidence of the broad strip of river bank which gave access to the works and the small cottages occupied by the millworkers. According to John Tweedie, in *A Water of Leith Walk*, the original Mossy Mill dates from the sixteenth century when it was a waulk mill owned by the brothers Mosie from whom the modern name is derived. In the early nineteenth century the mill was acquired by the McWhirter family who owned the bleachfields at Inglis Green near Slateford, and in 1838 it was converted to a paper mill. Although Mossy Mill closed in 1972, there are several remnants of the water-wheel age a few yards upstream. The weir which served the mill is in good condition with the lade being taken off on the south bank. Parts of the entrance sluice, relief sluice and winding gear have survived, but the lade, well constructed for a few hundred yards,

SNUFF MILL, JUNIPER GREEN.

Watt's Snuff Mill was on the north side of the track, a few hundred yards to the east of Juniper Green Station. The spur line, seen in the photograph, went to a small goods yard at the rear of the station. Nothing remains of the old mill building which was still producing snuff in the 1930s.

disappears completely as it enters the old mill complex. Mossy House, a handsome stone-built residence of uncertain date, previously occupied by the mill owner, stands high on the bank in attractive wooded policies, within sight of the concrete viaduct carrying the City Bypass across the Water of Leith. The walkway passes beneath the Bypass, the concrete pillars of which are spoiled by graffiti at ground level.

Beyond the Bypass, in the open landscape created at the time of the road-building programme, Woodhall Grain Mill operates on the north bank under the name of Alexander Inglis & Son Ltd., Grain and Agricultural Merchants. This was the approximate site of Curriemuir Mill, previously named Denholm's Mill in the early eighteenth century, and once the home of Hunter's Famous Lothian Oatmeal in the late nineteenth century. The modern works owned by Inglis is one of the few working mills in the valley, which was also provided with a greatly improved access road when the Bypass was built. There is no evidence of the original water power within any of the buildings, but two hundred yards upstream, beside the timber fencing on the left, some hewn stones mark the position of the weir. On the north bank, below a rocky promontory, the lade began its journey to Inglis Mill.

The next place of interest is probably the one where the greatest imagination is required to unravel its past as so little remains. It is at the point where the walkway is carried on a short stone bridge, with tubular metal handrails, across a shallow gulley in which there is an unusual arrangement of stone channels. This is the site of Watt's Snuff Mill, known to have been the last snuff manufacturer in the valley. John Mackay, writing in the *Evening News* in 1967, recalled when the snuff mill was a going concern in the 1930s. The Water of Leith drove a system of gear wheels to rotate the rollers for grinding, and to shake the sieve in the production of three main blends – Black, Brown and Imperial Snuff. Watt's Mill, which ceased production around 1940, and another one for grain a few yards upstream (Wright's Mill), were also known as Woodhall Bank Mills, but nothing remains of the buildings now. There is evidence of the stone channels below the bridge which carried the spent water from Watt's Snuff Mill back into the Water of Leith. The two-storey mill sat on the north side of the railway track with the basement below the level of the railway line. The lade entered from the west along the north side of the track where there was a branch to a goods yard siding. A signal box was built north-east of the mill and a tall signal mast was erected on the south side of the track.

West of Watt's Snuff Mill site is a large brick-built warehouse, once owned by the G. P. Inveresk Corporation, part of which is built on the site of the former Juniper Green railway station and its sidings. Accommodation for passengers was quite modest, consisting of one long narrow building with a flat roof and scalloped eaves, on the north side of the track. Behind it was a larger open shed built across the goods train siding. Access for pedestrians and vehicles was by the steep Station Brae from Lanark Road.

Immediately west of the station site, where the walkway forks, little remains of the once spectacular curved weir which served Watt's Snuff Mill and Wright's Grain Mill via a long lade which ran at the back of the railway goods yard. The blocked-up culvert can still be seen below the level of the fork in the walkway. The left-hand path leads to the site of the former Woodhall Board Mill, once one of the largest mill complexes in the valley. The extensive site between the walkway and the Water of Leith was levelled several years ago except for one or two rudimentary buildings along the north side. At the apex of this

Juniper Green Station *c.* 1906. The single-track railway line was opened by the Caledonian Railway Company on 1st August 1874 from Slateford to Balerno, with stations at Colinton, Juniper Green and Currie. Passenger services ceased on 30th October 1943 but goods trains used the line until the 1960s.

triangular site the weir and sluice gates are still evident. Woodhall Board Mill began life as a lint mill in the early eighteenth century, but, as the name suggests, it moved into the manufacture of paper and cardboard packaging.

After a gradual left-hand curve at the back of what was Veitch's Garden Centre, the walkway again crosses the Water of Leith by a rather curious bridge laid with lengths of timber on top of the normal walking surface. On the far side of the bridge the Water of Leith is seen on the right passing very close to an old house, the ground floor of which is protected by a substantial stone embankment on the north side. This is one of the old mill houses beside the ruin of East Mill

Bank Mill, owned by James Watt at the end of the eighteenth century. On the south bank, lying between the walkway and the Water of Leith, was East Mill Grain Mill and East Mill Snuff Mill. All the mill buildings have disappeared but there are remains of the weir and lade outflow just west of the bridge. Photographs taken at the beginning of the twentieth century show the very distinctive construction of East Mill Snuff Mill built high on the south bank with part of its structure protruding precariously on timber supports towards the river. A small wooden pedestrian bridge linking East Mill Bank Mill and East Mill Snuff Mill has long since disappeared. Also demolished are the steadings of Wyllie's Farm on the south bank which provided ponies for local Gala days, and theatrical events in Edinburgh.

A few hundred yards west of the bridge at East Mill Bank Mill are the massive buttresses of a much older bridge. This ancient structure, previously known as Mutter's Bridge, carries Blinkbonny Road over the lade, the walkway and the Water of Leith, supported on a series of arches of various sizes. On the outside of each parapet, within an oval-shaped recess, is the inscription:

BUILT BY
GENERAL
THOMAS SCOTT
OF MALLENY
1831

Beyond, the walkway continues to Currie and Balerno.

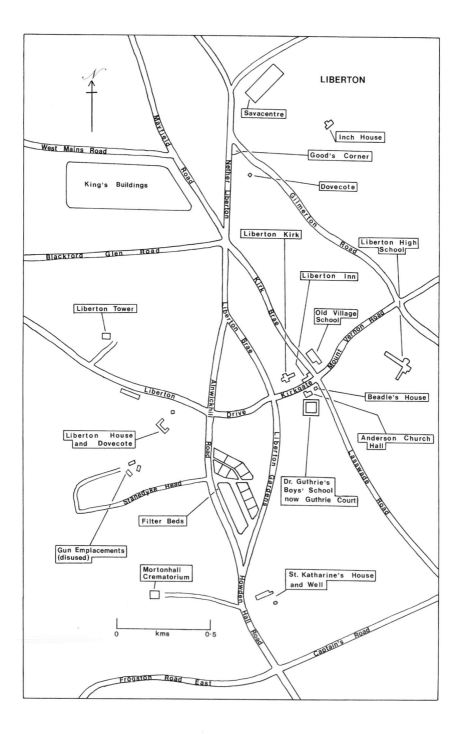

CHAPTER FOUR

Liberton

Liberton is perhaps one of the most elusive villages on the south side of Edinburgh in that it is possible, even today, to identify four separate communities within Liberton. The most important, by position and reputation, is Kirk Liberton, which grew up around the old church at the head of Kirk Brae. Half a mile to the west, Over Liberton or Upper Liberton came to prominence through the Littles of Liberton who resided, firstly, in the defensive Liberton Tower, and later in the much more elegant Liberton House. Two other communities to the north complete the group: Liberton Dams nestles at the foot of Liberton Brae, and Nether Liberton is clustered around the junction of Gilmerton Road and Craigmillar Park. All four, although distinct in themselves, came within the parish of Liberton and have in many ways developed along similar lines. The way that development has taken place is what makes Liberton historically interesting.

The origin of the name 'Liberton' is beset with problems. The usual explanation is that it is a corruption of Leperton or Lepertown, from a hospital for lepers which is said to have stood in the district. There are two objections to this, however. The first is that no trace has ever been found of a hospital in the district which admitted people suffering from leprosy. The second is even more convincing: the name Liberton or Libberton, as a surname, existed in the district for more than a hundred years before known outbreaks of the disease in Edinburgh. Stuart Harris, the eminent authority on place names in Edinburgh, goes even further. In *The Place Names of Edinburgh* Mr Harris states that the leper town explanation 'is not only fanciful but impossible, since the place name is much older than any use of the word "leper" or "lipper" in Scots'. According to Mr Harris, the name has an Anglian source in the old words for barley farm on the slope.

Liberton Kirk, designed by the eminent architect James Gillespie Graham, was built in 1815 on the site of an earlier church which had been damaged by fire. *Photograph by John Gill.*

THE VILLAGE WALKS

As the various Liberton locations are fairly far apart, each area has been taken in turn so that the places of historical interest closest to one another can be studied together. Kirk Liberton is dealt with first; then Upper Liberton (or Over Liberton) and St Katherine's; and finally Liberton Dams and Nether Liberton.

Kirk Liberton

Kirk Liberton, as the name suggests, is that part of the parish of Liberton situated around the old church. In this small area all the main elements of village life were located. The old approach to the village was by Kirk Brae to the crossroads at the junction of Lasswade Road, Mount Vernon Road and Kirkgate. The school was in the building now owned by Liberton Inn; the church and manse occupied a large area of ground to the north-west; and the village smiddy was on the north-east corner of Kirk Brae and Mount Vernon Road. Altogether it was a very compact community with most of the outlying district under cultivation. At the time of the *New Statistical Account of Scotland*, written in 1839, the picture painted by the Rev. James Begg was still one of a rural parish with thirty-four farms varying in size from 40 to 268 acres, many of them adopting a five-year crop rotation of potatoes, wheat, barley, grass and oats. Most of the living accommodation was abysmal with cottages on some farms in worse condition than the stables. Substantial improvement was evident by 1880, however, when Grant was able to say in *Old and New Edinburgh* that 'the parish itself has a thousand attractions, and is dressed out in neatness of enclosures, profusion of garden grounds, opulence of cultivation, elegance or tidiness of mansion, village and cottage, and busy stir and enterprise, which indicate full consciousness of the immediate vicinity of the proudest metropolis in Europe'. In the early part of the twentieth century the transformation of rural Liberton into a busy suburb was quite gradual up to the end of the Second World War. Post-war development absorbed many acres of ground previously used as farm land.

One of the most recent authoritative accounts of Liberton Kirk is contained in *Annals of Liberton* by the Rev. Campbell Ferenbach, minister of the parish from 1942 to 1970. Mr Ferenbach reviewed the scant evidence of the church's early history which can be traced back to a twelfth-century charter in the reign of David I. Although the exact age of old Liberton Kirk is not known, there have been several useful descriptions of it over the years. The Rev. Thomas Whyte, writing in 1792, said:

> The main entry to the church is on the south under a porch. The steeple at the west end makes a decent and venerable appearance. The spire or cupola was formerly of wood; in August 1744 it was struck by lightening (sic); it is now of stone. The bell here, as the inscription bears, was made by Henderson and Ormiston 1747. It is far superior to any in the neighbouring country parishes; but not at all like the former. The former was heard at Soutra-hill no less than sixteen miles distant.

This interesting old building reached the end of its useful lifetime in 1814 when it was demolished owing to damage by fire and the effects of old age. The 1747 bell was incorporated in the tower of the new church, built in 1815, exactly on the site of the old one. The new church, designed by the eminent architect, James Gillespie Graham, has been described, in Groome's *Ordnance Gazetteer of Scotland*, as a handsome semi-Gothic edifice. The very distinctive west tower, with

The bell, which hangs in the tower of Liberton Kirk, is still rung every Sunday morning. It was transferred from the old church building when the present church was built in 1815.

its corbelled parapet and four slender pinnacles, is a prominent land-mark seen from several viewpoints. The main body of the church is rectangular but its symmetrical walls are interrupted by graceful win-dows and several doorways. The foundation stone was laid on 27th January 1815 in the presence of the minister, the Rev. James Grant, the heritors and many of the parishioners.

Although the exterior of the church remains unaltered from Gillespie Graham's original work, the interior has been rearranged on more than one occasion. In 1882 the opportunity was taken to reduce the size of the original gallery which had extended round three sides of the church and tended to project too far. In 1958 the number of seats was reduced to nine hundred when more space was created in front of the commu-nion table for baptisms and marriages. The pulpit was retained on the south wall. Two very different memorials honour previous ministers: on the west wall an ornate group in stone commemorates the Rev. William Purdie whose 'short but eminently useful ministry' was from 26th January 1832 until his death on 16th November 1834; and on the east wall a small bronze plaque commemorates the Rev. John Spence Ewen D.D., minister of Liberton Kirk from 1928 to 1941. The Baird Vault on the north-east corner is accessible, and contains several ornate marble stones commemorating various members of the Baird family.

When Liberton Kirk was built in 1815, pipe organs were unheard of. It was not until 1884 that the idea of a harmonium was mooted, but following objections, it was not installed until more than a year later, and even then was used at evening services only. It was not until 9th January 1890 that full agreement was reached to use the harmonium at all services. Seventeen years later, on 11th March 1907, the same problem arose again when it was suggested that a pipe organ be installed. Opposition delayed the 'yes' vote until April 1914, by which time the First World War put an end to any such expenditure. Event-ually, an Ingram two-manual pedal organ was installed in 1930 and operated for more than forty years before being replaced in 1972 by a digital Allan organ.

The church halls, beadle's house and manse are all within a short distance of the church. On the south side of Kirkgate the Anderson Church Hall, with an imposing wheel window to the north, was erected in 1888, partly by public subscription and partly from a grant made by the Trustees of the late Miss Anderson of Moredun. An additional small hall was built in 1929 and a further hall was built in 1954 in response to the increased population in the district. The property on the south-west corner of Kirkgate and Lasswade Road was acquired in 1956 and named Kirk House. Following a lengthy fundraising venture, a two-storey building was erected linking Kirk House and the Anderson Hall. The new complex, named Kirk Centre, was opened in October 1993. The original manse dates from before 1701 but shortly after the new Liberton Kirk was built another manse was erected in 1821. This was a handsome square Georgian house situated in three and a half acres of ground to the north of the church. It was sold for redevelopment in 1960, along with most of the garden ground, and a new manse was built on the remaining piece of ground.

The old kirkyard which surrounds Liberton Parish Church has many interesting old stones. On the outside of the south wall of the church is a Gothic memorial, enclosed by a small railing, erected by the parishioners, to commemorate the Rev. James Grant, minister of the parish from 1789 to 1831. On the left-hand side of the path, which leads from the kirkyard entrance to the bell tower, two contrasting stones have only the surname in common. The first is a tiny plain stone with the epitaph 'A man is best known when he is dead' on one side, and 'Jas. Taylor' chiselled across the rounded top. Within a few yards of this modest gravestone is a ten-feet-high ornate pedimented stone to James Baxter Taylor of Gilmerton who died on 6th June 1737. The west wall also contains several stones set into the boundary wall: a wall stone with a finialled mantleshelf to Robert Bryden, Portioner in Greenend, 1.4.1819; and a tall pedimented and pillared tomb for John Nicol who died on 17.3.1765, and his wife Helen. Perhaps the most unusual tomb lies midway between the west boundary wall and the west door to the bell tower: that of William Stratton of Tower Farm, 1754, whose effigy reposes beneath the tablestone. Elaborate detail includes a panel on the west side depicting ploughing, furrowing and sowing. On the east wall the arrangement of stones is similar to the west wall. No one here could fail to see KELLY in large bold lettering on a white slab for Thomas Johnstone Kelly, schoolmaster of Liberton, who died on 9th December 1876. Nearby lies Robert Stevenson, Surgeon, of Gilmerton, the Founder and President of Gilmerton Library. Liberton Kirk and its ancient Kirkyard are included in the publication *Churches to Visit in Scotland*.

Pupils at Liberton Primary School in Mount Vernon Road in 1960, a few years before the school closed in 1965. *Courtesy of Jean Murray.*

A group of children involved in outdoor play, in 1998, at Liberton Nursery School which occupies the building previously used as Liberton Primary School in Mount Vernon Road. The ground floor of the building was the original 'village' school until 1898 when a second storey was added. *Photograph by Mrs Eileen Sharp, Head Teacher.*

Traditionally, the village school is frequently located near to the parish church, and Liberton is no exception. One of the earliest accounts of a school in the village was again by the Rev. Thomas Whyte in 1792. Although Mr Whyte did not describe the actual school in his report, it is known to have been the building on the north corner of Kirk Brae and Kirkgate, presently occupied by Liberton Inn, part of which is named after Reuben Butler, the schoolmaster in Scott's *Heart of Midlothian*. By 1873 Liberton School Board had opened a new school in a single-storey building on the north side of Mount Vernon Road. The modest accommodation was extended in 1879, 1886 and 1898, by which time the roll had reached 240 pupils. With the minimum of administrative delay, the school closed early for the summer holidays on 30th June 1898, and nine weeks later the pupils returned to find that their old building had been given another storey containing two extra classrooms. In the 1960s the building was still heated by open coal fires, the total roll had been reduced to about eighty pupils, and, because of the lack of space, gymnastic sessions were held in the church hall in Kirkgate. The school continued in the same building until 2nd July 1965, the final log book entry being: 'Today Liberton Primary School ceases to exist as such. It has always been a happy place with a family spirit and it is hoped that one day children's voices will again be heard within its walls'. That time was not long in coming. In 1967 the building was renovated and opened as Liberton Nursery School which still operates morning and afternoon sessions for more than one hundred pre-school age children.

Dr Guthrie's Boys' School was also at Liberton on the west side of Lasswade Road, only a few hundred yards from Liberton Primary School. The plain Gothic building in pink and red sandstone was designed in 1885 by Sydney Mitchell, and opened in 1888, fifteen years after the death of its founder. Biographical notes on Dr Guthrie appear in the chapter on Gilmerton where the corresponding Girls' School was opened in 1904. Dr Guthrie was born in Brechin in 1803 but it was not until after the Disruption in 1843 that he set himself the task of improving the education and living standards of hundreds of children in and around the Cowgate in Edinburgh. His vision is usually traced to an event which occurred one day when he was strolling with a friend in Holyrood Park near St Anthony's Well. The habit had grown up of young boys and girls congregating at the well where they offered to

Indian Club Drill at Dr Guthrie's Industrial School for Boys in Liberton, 1908. The school building was designed in 1885 by Sydney Mitchell and was opened in 1888. The corresponding Girls' School at Gilmerton was opened in 1904.

Bringing in the harvest at Little Road with Liberton Gardens in the background, 1949. *Courtesy of Mr & Mrs Philp*.

supply to any passer-by a cup of cool, refreshing spring water for a ha'penny. In conversation with the children, Dr Guthrie asked if they would go to school if they were also fed, to which one young boy answered: 'Ay will I sir, and bring the haill land, too', meaning, of course, all the children in the stair or tenement. Eventually a soup kitchen was started in a basement room of Dr Guthrie's church, Free St John's, but it was necessary to make a specific appeal to the public, in the *First Plea for the Ragged Schools*, before the idea gained ground. The *Second Plea* contained statistical information in support of the original idea: in 1851 the Ragged Schools claimed over two hundred successes and a marked reduction in the number of children in prison or openly begging in the streets. The movement was given impetus by the Education Act of 1872 and developed through the system of Approved Schools, replaced in 1969 by List D Schools. After Dr Guthrie's at Liberton was closed around 1982, the building was redeveloped in 1986 to provide residential and care homes, now under the name Guthrie Court.

Over Liberton and St Katherine's

George Good, in *Liberton in Ancient and Modern Times*, describes the barony of Upper or Over Liberton as extending 'from the Braid Burn on the north to the boundary of the Mortonhall estate on the south, and from the Braids on the west to a point beyond Liberton Church, including what is called Lesley Park and that piece of ground which belongs to the poor of the parish, on the east'. The old hamlet of Over Liberton, as distinct from the barony, was never more than a handful of houses and farm steadings, huddled around two principal buildings: to the west stood the ancient, high-walled fortress of Liberton Tower; and to the east, at the end of a long tree-lined avenue, lay Liberton House. At the present day, Liberton Tower lies to the north of Liberton Drive and Liberton House lies to the south.

In the sixteenth century, the barony of Over Liberton was gradually acquired by the Little family. In 1528 the previous owners, the Dalmahoys, granted a merk of land to Clement Little, burgess of Edinburgh, and in 1587 Alexander Dalmahoy sold another part of the land to William Little, whose descendants eventually acquired the whole barony. The Littles were a strong and influential family whose interest in the land has continued to the present day through the Little Gilmours.

Clement Little, who acquired the first interest in 1528, had two sons, Clement Little, the advocate, and William Little, merchant and later Lord Provost of Edinburgh. Clement, the advocate, was a man of considerable intellect, who gifted several hundred books to form the nucleus of a library for Edinburgh University. He died on 1st April 1580 and was buried in Greyfriars Kirkyard. Less well known, now, was his younger brother, William Little, Lord Provost of Edinburgh from 1585 to 1587 and again in 1591. William died in 1601 and was buried beside his brother in Greyfriars. The family tomb might have remained relatively obscure but for the efforts of William Little's great-grandson, who erected an imposing monument over the site of the grave in 1683 in memory of his great-grandfather, WILLIAM LITTLE OF OVER LIBERTON. This huge structure on the south wall of Greyfriars Kirkyard, resembling a four-poster bed in stone, consists of ten Corinthian columns on chamfered pedestals, supporting a massive roof, on each corner of which is an elegant female figure looking out over the graveyard. Within the pillars, a serene recumbent effigy faces the churchyard exit, with not a hint of the malicious rumours which compelled James Brown, in 1867, to include a special note in the Appendix to *The Epitaphs and Monumental Inscriptions in Greyfriars Churchyard*:

> Little's Tomb, on the South Wall – An impression has got hold of the popular mind that the four female figures on the top of this tomb represent four daughters who poisoned their father, who is supposed to be the reclining figure in the centre of the tomb. We need scarcely add that this is pure fiction, without the least semblance of truth in it. The figures are emblems of Justice, Mercy, Peace and Love.

The high-walled fortress of Liberton Tower stands, surrounded by buildings of considerable antiquity, a few hundred yards north of Liberton Drive, almost opposite the private road leading to Meadowhead Farm. The tower was built in the fifteenth century by the Dalmahoy family who eventually sold out to the Littles. An excellent description of the building is given in the Edinburgh volume of *The Buildings of Scotland*. Subsequent renovations, carried out in 1997 and 1998, have greatly enhanced the building without significantly altering its basic construction. The original plan was a four-storey rectangular block, thirty-five feet long, twenty-five feet wide, and rising forty-five

Left: The tall fifteenth-century Liberton Tower, photographed from the north-west in 1997, before extensive restoration by the architects, Simpson & Brown. *Courtesy of Simpson & Brown, Architects.*

Right: Liberton Tower, in 1998, beautifully restored, and now in use as holiday accommodation let by Country Cottages in Scotland. *Courtesy of Simpson & Brown, Architects.*

feet to a pitched roof of stone slabs surrounded by a parapet walk. The construction was harled rubble with dressed stone at the windows, doors and corners. When the Littles moved out of Liberton Tower to Liberton House around 1600, the old building entered a long period of gradual decline, not effectively arrested until very recently. Although the roof had remained reasonably watertight, the walls had begun to deteriorate and all interior timber had been removed. In 1992 the Liberton Trust granted a 100-year lease of the tower, with some adjoining land, to the Castles of Scotland Preservation Trust. Assisted by a grant from the Architectural Heritage Fund, the Castles of Scotland Preservation Trust commissioned a feasibility study which examined three possible uses for Liberton Tower – as a museum, as an office or for holiday letting. The third option was chosen, mainly on the basis that it would involve the least alteration to the original structure. The promise of financial support from the Heritage Lottery Fund and Historic Scotland enabled the builder, Ian Cumming, to begin work in January 1997 under the direction of the Edinburgh architects, Simpson & Brown.

As the whole interior of the tower had disappeared over the years, a lot of investigative work was required before work began. Considerable assistance was gained from the meticulous survey done by MacGibbon & Ross, who included a description of Liberton Tower in *The Castellated and Domestic Architecture of Scotland*, first published in 1887. The two timber floors had to be reconstructed, maintaining the original horizontal division into four main storeys, with a fifth storey rediscovered in the roof space at the level of the door to the parapet. The two floors below the lower vaulted ceiling were reinstated, the upper one to house a modern kitchen and bathroom, and the lower one (with its restricted headroom) to contain the heating boiler. The main hall, on the third storey, was completely renovated, retaining many of the original features, including the fireplace, the garderobes and the Laird's Lug, or listening hole, originally designed to be used from the north stair. The vaulted area above the main hall still contained two fireplaces and two staircases, suggesting two separate rooms, but the floors had long since been removed. The position of the original partition between the two rooms was evident from the fact that only one pair of upper and lower beams coincided. Further investigative work revealed the small fifth storey which has now been used to house the water tank.

In addition to the restoration work on the tower, a comprehensive survey was made of the entire site by the archaeologist, Thomas Addyman. The draw hole above the main door was discovered, putting beyond doubt the belief that access to the door (above ground level) had been by a drawbridge. This would have been lowered to a timber or stone stair, standing apart from the main tower, but no doubt well within firing range from the parapets. Unfortunately, no clear evidence of the stair's foundation was traced, but a well, a pavement and the position of buildings to the north-west of the tower were revealed.

On completion of the work in April 1998, the interior was furnished in a late medieval and Scottish seventeenth-century character, without any claim to authenticity, but greatly enhancing its new use as holiday accommodation let by Country Cottages in Scotland.

To the south-east, Liberton House lies at the end of an avenue of elm trees, a few hundred yards south of Liberton Drive. The entrance is marked by twin gate pillars, unusually close together, supporting tall ornamental iron gates bearing the letters LH in gold. The driveway leads past a seventeenth-century doocot on the west side, and ends in a courtyard formed by two aspects of the main house and a two-storey addition built slightly later as servants' quarters.

The exact age of Liberton House is uncertain although the best-informed opinion places it in the late sixteenth century. It was built for the Littles of Liberton who were previously resident in the much plainer Liberton Tower. During its four centuries, the house has been altered on numerous occasions so that its layout is now rather confusing. Its L-plan has three storeys in the main block and four storeys in the wing, with a round stair tower formed within the angle, and corbelled out to become square-shaped at the second floor. The numerous windows are generally small and there are gun loops overlooking the principal entrance, previously enclosed by a stone porch built about 1840. Extensive restoration work was done around 1890 by the tenant, Godfrey Cunninghame, Advocate, and in 1936 Rowand Anderson, Paul and Partners restored the wallhead with late seventeenth-century style dormers after removing a Georgian top floor.

Like many similar dwellings, Liberton House has several date stones which enhance its appearance but confound the historian. On the south-east corner there is a sundial, round the top of which is the motto: AS.THE.SVNE.RVNS.SO.DEATH.COMES. Above the dial is a carved scroll containing the arms of the Littles, the initials WL for William Little, and the date 1683, this being the year when the commemorative tomb was erected in Greyfriars Kirkyard. The most intriguing stone, however, is older than the house itself and has been re-sited over a doorway in the two-storey west extension. This lintel stone, bearing the inscription WILLIAME – 1570 – LITIL, prompted the authors of the Edinburgh volume of *The Buildings of Scotland* to question where the stone had come from. As the lintel stone is positioned immediately below a much larger square, moulded stone with the initials WL, the answer may well be contained in an interesting account given by Wilson in *Memorials of Edinburgh in the Olden Times*. At page 220 of Volume I Wilson says: 'On the east side of an open court, immediately beyond the Roman Eagle Hall (in the Cowgate) stood the ancient mansion of the Littles of Craigmillar, bearing on a large moulded and deeply recessed stone panel the name of one of the old city worthies: WILLIAME – 1570 – LITIL'.

Unfortunately Liberton House suffered serious damage in a fire in June 1991 as a result of which the roof and upper floors of the main house were completely destroyed. The remainder of the house was also damaged by water used to extinguish the blaze. Subsequently, damp conditions, caused principally by the theft of slates from the lower roofs, resulted in an extensive outbreak of dry rot which destroyed much of the Victorian interior. Fortunately, the desolate shell of the once-proud Liberton House was noticed by the architects, Nicholas and Limma Groves-Raines, who recognised the potential for renovation, having completed similar work at Peffermill House in 1981 and at Edinample Castle in the late 1980s. With financial assistance from Historic Scotland provisional work started in October 1993. In the main house all the nineteenth-century timber and plasterwork was stripped out to reveal the original wall finishes and layout. The Arts and Crafts studded doors to the main rooms and the stair well were salvaged, along with the original oak and pine beams at the first floor, and the remains of earlier timbers in the attic floor. The Victorian entrance porch was removed completely on the basis that its appearance was not in keeping with the remainder of the restored house. Conservation work is still to be undertaken on the 1892 painted ceiling by Thomas Bonnar Jnr., and on the original kitchen on the ground floor.

There are also plans to return the garden to its former glory by the creation of parterres and topiary, and replanting an orchard and wild garden. The doocot, to the west of the main driveway, is rectangular with a lean-to roof of slate, walls of stone with harling, and crow-stepped gables. It measures approximately twenty-two feet by twenty feet and is entered by a door in the centre of the south wall above which is a circular light. The birds enter by two rows of ten holes in a shallow dormer window in the slated roof. The interior, which is

Liberton House, dating from the late sixteenth century, was extensively damaged by fire in June 1991, but was subsequently restored by the architects, Nicholas Groves-Raines. *Photograph by Nicholas Groves-Raines.*

still in excellent condition, has twenty-four tiers on the high north wall, and a decreasing number on the sloping east and west walls, providing more than a thousand nesting places.

No respectable Scottish house of comparable antiquity is without its ghost, and Liberton House is no exception. An apparition is said to have appeared on numerous occasions over the years in a variety of forms, one of which was reproduced in *The Scotsman* on 17th June 1936 along with a letter from David Hunter Blair who possessed the original photograph taken at Liberton House, in which 'a large and extraordinarily sinister human face appeared with handsome features and a smile as enigmatic as that of Mona Lisa'. The original photograph has not been traced but the newspaper reproduction, with its consequent reduction in quality, is disappointing. Tradition has it that the ghost has appeared in at least three different guises: Pierre, a French nobleman, with a propensity to startle the occupants by whistling when least expected, especially near the doocot; a female member of the Little family who was imprisoned in Edinburgh for assisting the Covenanters; and a Cavalier in costume and headgear of the seventeenth century, believed to be the one whose photograph appeared in *The Scotsman*. Even the fire in 1991 does not appear to have extinguished the ghost completely. Although no 'sightings' have been reported in recent years, voices have been heard and electrical apparatus has malfunctioned without any obvious human intervention.

To reach St Katherine's Well from Liberton House, turn right, off Liberton Drive, into Alnwickhill Road, previously known as Stanedyke-head. The most dominant stone building on the west side of the road was the Edinburgh Industrial Home for Fallen Women, built in 1891, but now in private residential use.

To the east, several acres of land, bounded by Alnwickhill Road, Liberton Gardens and Liberton Drive, house the reservoir and filter beds for the public supply of water to the east side of Edinburgh. This extensive arrangement of reservoirs and filter beds operates on a simple gravity system without the need for electrically driven pumps. Water reaches the main raw water reservoir of twenty million gallons from the Tala, Crawley and Moorfoot pipes and then falls by gravity to each of twelve slow sand filter beds, before entering the two clearwater storage tanks of five million gallons each. There is an additional outflow on the main reservoir which can be used as an overflow. In typically Victorian style, the various dates and the names of the people involved in the construction of the scheme are listed on two ornate plaques on each side of the original Clear Water Tank House, built of good quality stone in the style of a small classical temple with a stone flagged roof. The scheme was first considered in 1873, opened in 1879, and finally completed in 1885 by J. & A. Leslie, Engineers. The reservoir and filter beds are not generally open to the public but the small 'classical temple' is clearly visible from Liberton Gardens.

Within a few hundred yards of the filter beds a much more ancient source of water, believed to have medicinal properties, can be found at the Balm Well of St Katherine. In relation to modern street names, the well is within the garden ground of St Katherine's House (now the Balmwell) on the east side of Howden Hall Road almost opposite the entrance to Mortonhall Crematorium.

The age of the well is uncertain, but according to tradition it was established by St Catherine of Alexandria who brought the precious oil from Mount Sinai to Scotland, some of which now floats on the surface of the water. The better opinion is that the black tarry substance on the water is produced from the bituminous shale beds at Burdiehouse and Straiton. Whatever its origins, it has been commented upon by several eminent writers over the years and has benefited from Royal patronage on more than one occasion. In 1504 James IV made an offering to 'Sanct Katrine's of the oly well' and in 1617 James VI ordered 'that it should be built with stones from the bottom to the top and that a door and a pair of steps be made for it that men might have the more easy access to the bottom to get the balm'. Unfortunately, the King's refurbishment was completely destroyed by Cromwell's troops in 1650. Perhaps the most comprehensive account of the well is contained in *Stones and Curiosities of Edinburgh and Neighbourhood* by Dr George A. Fothergill. The author's medical background compels him to point out 'that the corpulent, overfed hunting man, whose body may be subject to eczema, is recommended by his physician to eat less and hunt more', rather than surrender his malady to the powers of the oily water:

> Some went to St. Katherine's Well
> That magical, wonderful well,
> To be rid of their bigness –
> Preternatural bigness –
> Their burden of beef –
> In the full belief
> They'd be quit of their sickness
> And return as sound as a bell.

After his humorous start Dr Fothergill goes on to review in depth the early references and to describe the lintel stone which bears the date 1563 and the initials A and P on either side of an unknown coat of arms. It has been suggested that the initials relate to the Prestons of Craigmillar or Alexander de Pardouin of Newbattle.

In recent years the well was allowed to fall into serious disrepair, but in 1995 it was repaired and protected by a light fence. Unfortunately, further vandalism has occurred. The Balm Well is in the garden ground of the former St Katherine's House which has recently been acquired as a restaurant and public bar. The house, originally designed by John Simpson for his own use, and built by David Bell in 1806, has been altered on several occasions over the years. The castellated north front probably belonged to the original plan with the south-facing rooms and new entrance hall added shortly thereafter. To the east of the main house, the stable block has survived almost intact. It includes stables, a lean-to style doocot, a horse gin (with its open sides now bricked up) and a range of workshops which at one time would have been a hive of activity at the hub of a small country estate. Tradition has it that the body of St Katherine lies buried below one of the concrete floors with only a rusting laundry boiler as a headstone!

Nether Liberton; Liberton Dams

Nether Liberton lies at the junction of Craigmillar Park and Gilmerton Road. Its origins are traced by George Good to at least 1143. Although direct references are not numerous, *Charters and Documents relating to the City of Edinburgh 1143–1540* refers to an Indenture dated 29th November 1387 'between Adam Forester, Laird of Nether Liberton, and the Provost and the Community of Edinburgh on the one part and certain masons on the other in regard to building five chapels on the south side of the parish church of Edinburgh'. The population probably reached its peak in the late eighteenth century when there was a community of about three hundred people. There was a village cross, a weekly market, a school, a schoolhouse, and a schoolmaster. The two main occupations were brewing and milling, both of which relied heavily upon the water of the Braid Burn. One of the mill buildings, at Old Mill Lane, is still extant with the remains of its iron wheel visible on the south wall. Perhaps the part of Nether Liberton best known is Good's Corner at the north-west end of Gilmerton Road. For many years the old buildings were used as a sawmill and joiner's shop by the Good family.

On Gilmerton Road, a few hundred yards south of Good's Corner, is Nether Liberton doocot dating from the fifteenth or sixteenth century. It was probably built by the proprietors of Inch House, on the east

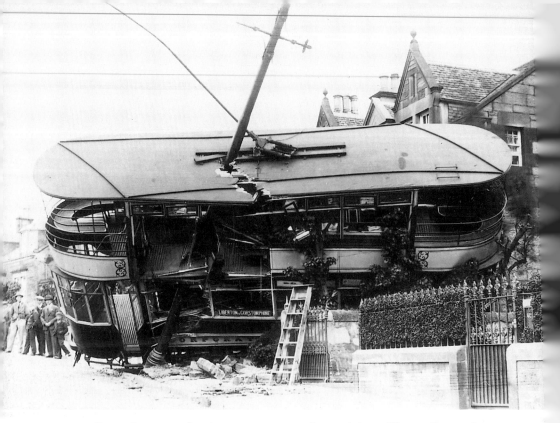

On 1st June 1929 electric car 349 ran out of control down Liberton Brae and came to rest in the garden of one of the houses. Fortunately, no one was injured. *Courtesy of A. W. Brotchie.*

Braefoot, at the foot of Liberton Brae, in 1917. The small building on the right, then occupied by H. & T. Moonie, Plumbers & Slaters, was demolished many years ago. The small sign appears to be for A. & J. Macnab, Dyers & Cleaners, of Inglis Green.

The old iron mill wheel, photographed at Nether Liberton in 1986, was in operation in the nineteenth century when the mill was owned by Andrew Dick. *Photograph by Graham C. Cant.*

side of the main road. The dovecot is believed to be the largest in Edinburgh, built on the lean-to, or lectern, principle, with two main chambers, each with its own heavily protected doorway. All the internal walls have nesting boxes totalling two thousand and seventy-two.

Inch House, now a Community Centre, lies to the east of Gilmerton Road. The earliest date on the house is 1617 when the property belonged to James Winram whose descendant George Winram became a Lord of Session in 1649, taking the title Lord Liberton. Originally the house was L-shaped in plan, three storeys and an attic in height with a square five-storey stair turret in the angle. James Winram added a two-storey extension to the north in 1634, and in 1660 the house was acquired by the Gilmours of Craigmillar who added a west wing in the late eighteenth century. Extensive external and internal renovations were done in 1891 under the supervision of the architects MacGibbon & Ross.

Laurie's Map of 1766 shows Liberton Dams between Mayfield Road and Kirk Brae on the main route out of Edinburgh from Causewayside to Liberton. Liberton Brae and Craigmillar Park were not constructed until the road improvements of 1815, referred to on the outer parapet of the bridge across the Braid Burn. The inscription contains some unusual spelling:

> This improved access to
> the City of Edinburgh
> extending from Libberton
> Daams to Newington was
> executed by the trustees of
> the Laswade district
> Anno 1815

The Nether Liberton doocot, dating from the fifteenth or sixteenth century, is believed to be the largest in Edinburgh with more than two thousand nesting boxes. *Photograph by Phyllis M. Cant.*

Three young lads, in their Sunday best, aboard the cart used by the Greenend Dairy for milk deliveries. The date of the photograph and the names of the boys have not been discovered.

The Dams was the smallest of the four Liberton communities but was still large enough to have a school and mission hall up until about 1890. There was also a large dairy owned by the Laidlaw family on the triangular piece of ground to the east of Mayfield Road. A photograph reproduced in *The Print of his Shoe* by James Goodfellow, the missionary, shows Liberton Dams in the early 1900s. There are no villas yet at the south end of Mayfield Road, but among the old houses on the west side, opposite Laidlaw's Dairy, is a small general shop reached by a tiny stone bridge across the mill lade as it returns to the Braid Burn.

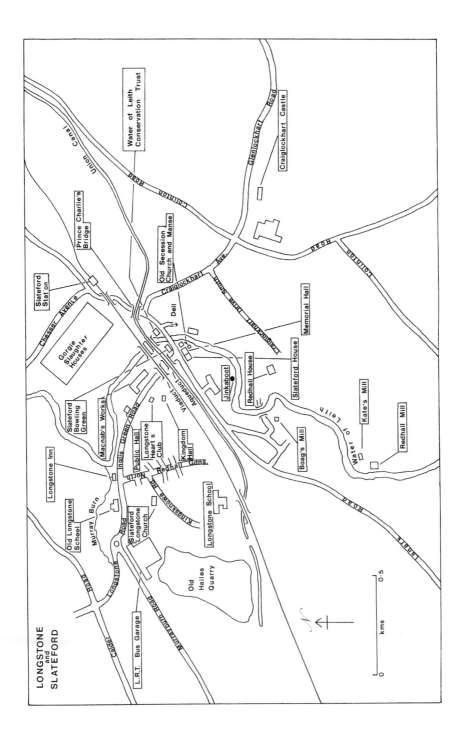

LONGSTONE and SLATEFORD

Union Canal
Chesser Avenue
Slateford Station
Prince Charlie's Bridge
Colinton Road
Water of Leith Conservation Trust
Glenlockhart Road
Craiglockhart Castle
Gorgie Slaughter Houses
Old Secession Church and Manse
Craiglockhart Ave.
Dell
Tradmonde Road
Colinton Road
Memorial Hall
Slateford Bowling Green
Macnab's Works
Jinkaboot
Redhall House
Slateford House
Kate's Mill
Redhall Mill
Longstone Inn
Inglis Green Road
Public Hall
Longstone Heart's Club
Kingdom Hall
Viaduct
Aqueduct
Redhall Gdns.
Boag's Mill
Water of Leith
North Union Rd
Murray Burn
Old Longstone School
Slateford Longstone Church
Kingsknowe Rd
Longstone School
Old Hailes Quarry
Lanark Road
Longstone Road
L.R.T. Bus Garage
Kingsknowe Road
Calder Road

kms
0   0·5

Longstone and Slateford

Longstone and Slateford lie within a few hundred yards of one another in the shallow-sided valley of the Water of Leith. The two villages grew up at different times for economic and topographical reasons which do not now have the same impact on the community. Whilst pockets of independence may yet exist, for the most part the villages remain separate in name only. Perhaps the greatest influence in breaking down any remaining barrier has been the influx of population in the peripheral housing estates, the inhabitants of which have not felt the need for specific affinity with one village or the other.

Longstone derives its name from a long stone which was once used as a bridge to cross the Murray Burn beside the right-of-way to Stenhouse Mill. Slateford, as the name implies, grew up around the ford, near the slaty outcrop of rock upstream from the bridge which carries Lanark Road over the Water of Leith. In the upper valley, several mills thrived on the good supply of water used for milling paper, corn, barley, snuff and spices, as early as the sixteenth century. Other mills were located on the lower reaches of the Water of Leith near the Murray Burn tributary at Longstone.

Over the years, road, rail and water transport have converged on Longstone and Slateford as the most convenient point at which to cross the Water of Leith. In 1818 the Union Canal was carried across the valley on a series of elegant stone arches, and in 1847 the railway viaduct followed the same line, but at a slightly lower level. The main road through Slateford has also been widened on numerous occasions in the past, the last of which removed many of the old houses on either side of the village street.

Electric tram service No. 4, at the terminus near Slateford Station in 1946,
ready for the return journey to Piershill.

A much earlier electric tram, probably converted from the previous cable car
system, on Slateford Road. The small sign, below the destination board,
reads 'SWING TROLLEY THIS SIDE'. The space for advertisements on the side
of the tram asks: 'Why is your Advertisement not on this Car?'.

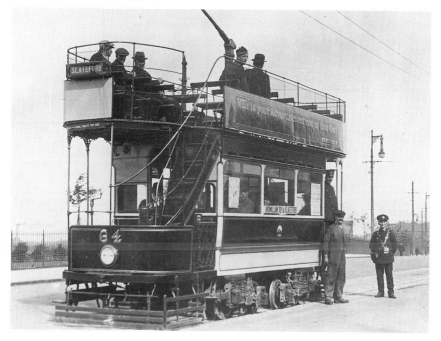

THE VILLAGE WALK

To visit the various places of interest, take either the orthodox route at street level, as per the map, or, alternatively, enjoy a 'bird's eye' view of the district from the towpath of the Union Canal as it crosses the valley of the Water of Leith. There are various access points to the canal towpath, but the nearest is from the north side of Lanark Road (near its junction with Craiglockhart Avenue) by the flight of wooden steps on the city-side of Prince Charlie's Bridge. A fairly steep climb, in one straight flight, takes us up to the level of the canal banks. Turn right at the head of the steps, where, a few hundred yards on, the canal narrows as it enters the aqueduct high above Lanark Road and Inglis Green Road. There is no access to the towpath on the south side of the aqueduct.

Looking south, it is possible to see most of Lanark Road running through the old village of Slateford. Originally the road was much

Slateford village before the various road improvements, with Back Row leading off to the left, the old stone bridge in the centre, and, on the right, the Cross Keys Inn and Slateford House. *From* Picturesque Views of Colinton and District.

Slateford
U.F. Manse

This building, described as Slateford United Free Manse, dates from 1785 when the Secession Church was also built. Both buildings are still extant, although in secular use, to the south-east of Lanark Road where it crosses over the Water of Leith.

narrower but a few decades ago many of the buildings on the north side of the road were demolished for the construction of a wider road and a new bridge over the Water of Leith. Much of the old village, near the junction with Craiglockhart Avenue, was demolished many years ago and is now occupied by a car saleroom and a garage. The remaining historical part of the south side is beyond the road bridge, beginning with the eighteenth-century Cross Keys Inn. The castellated gateway leads to the former Secession church and manse dating from 1785. The congregation was formed in 1782 primarily for parishioners from Corstorphine who objected to the introduction of the Paraphrases. For a time they met at Sighthill before acquiring the Slateford site as their permanent home. In 1783 the congregation was augmented by a group from Colinton, and later by a contingent of the Cameronian congregation from Old Pentland. The church took part in the various church unions in Scotland, becoming first United Presbyterian, and then United Free, before finally becoming part of the Church of Scotland in 1929. The congregation moved in 1955 to the new Slateford-Longstone Parish Church in Kingsknowe Road North. At the present day, the old

Secession church building is in commercial use and the two-storey manse, beside it, is a private house.

To the west of the castellated gateway is the Chalmers Memorial Hall, designed by the architect James Jerdan. The ornamental stonework above the doorway contains the initials DC for David Chalmers, and the date 1899, the year of his death. The hall, which communicated with the much older Slateford House to the west, was built by David Chalmers' widow Isabella Grace Grant Chalmers, for the purpose of carrying on 'home mission work in the village of Slateford and district in connection with the parish church of Craiglockhart'. The adjacent Slateford House, dating from around 1770, was, for long, associated with the Inglis family of Redhall. Margaret Inglis, the eldest daughter of David Inglis, a prosperous linen manufacturer and clothier, lived there for many years until her death in 1880.

The pitched roof of old Slateford School on the north side of Lanark Road can also be seen from the aqueduct. Records for the school are available from 1864 but it is clear that a school existed prior to that date on the same piece of ground. The school log books confirm that substantial rebuilding was planned in 1898. After the school closed in 1924 it was used from time to time for classes from Longstone School when extra space was needed. Between 1945 and 1952 it was used for the education of handicapped children transferred from St Nicholas School in Gorgie. At the present day it is the headquarters of the Water of Leith Conservation Trust, further details of which appear later in this chapter.

To the west of the former school building, the wide double-span, reinforced concrete bridge replaced, in 1967, a narrow three-arch stone bridge, supported by buttressed cutwaters and a separate culvert for the mill lade. Slateford Bowling Club still nestles below the canal aqueduct but the lade, which ran between the clubhouse and a row of old cottages, has long since been blocked off and filled in. All the old houses, including the Railway Inn, between the bowling green and Inglis Green Road, were demolished and replaced by modern dwellings.

The view to the north of the aqueduct is equally interesting. Running parallel, but at a lower level, is the 14-arch railway viaduct constructed in 1847. Beyond the viaduct, on the right-hand side of Inglis Green Road, are several industrial and commercial units on land formerly occupied by A. & J. Macnab Ltd., the famous cleaners and dyers. The area has a long association with the trade, stretching back to 1773 when George Inglis of Redhall leased an area of ground to Joseph Reid to be used as a bleachfield. The lease included Gray's Mill and the Haughs, below Slateford, on which Reid erected a bleaching house and a mill. After Reid became bankrupt in 1778 the dyeing business was revived by Hugh McWhirter, who was succeeded in 1849 by the Macnab brothers. Their name became synonymous with Inglis Green for more than a century. The business was later bought by Alex Stevenson, brother-in-law of the Macnab brothers, who kept the name A. & J. Macnab, working in close liaison with his own drapery shops. Many of the early processes and business dealings of the Macnabs are described in *A Company History* published privately in 1960.

During the Slateford and Longstone road improvements of 1967 Inglis Green Road was widened to occupy two railway arches, and a traffic roundabout was built at the junction with Lanark Road, almost

These cottages, on the east side of Inglis Green Road, *c.* 1917, were occupied by the employees of A. & J. Macnab, Cleaners & Dyers, whose extensive premises can be seen behind the cottages.

One of the old village hostelries, the Longstone Inn, photographed in 1986. Longstone derives its name from a long stone which was once used as a bridge to cross the Murray Burn at the back of the Inn. *Photograph by Phyllis M. Cant.*

opposite Slateford House. Prior to 1967 Inglis Green Road was very narrow, lined by cottages for the employees of A. & J. Macnab, and passed under only one of the railway arches. The village smiddy, and a group of small cottages in the form of a courtyard, stood on the west side between Lanark Road and the canal aqueduct. Inglis Green Road leads to the old village of Longstone, grouped around Longstone Inn at the confluence of the Murray Burn and the Water of Leith. It is here that the ancient 'long stone' provided a rudimentary crossing over the Murray Burn. A few hundred yards beyond the Inn is old Longstone School, dating from 1877, but greatly extended over the years, until 1956 when the new Longstone School was opened in Longstone Grove. Nearby, in Kingsknowe Road North, is Slateford-Longstone Parish Church, designed in 1954 by Leslie Grahame MacDougall, and described in the Edinburgh volume of *The Buildings of Scotland* as 'mildly Italian, the circular east tower seen as a light-flooded chancel from the portal-arched nave'.

Hailes Quarry, to the west of Longstone, has long since been filled

Longstone village, looking west towards Calder Road, showing many of the original buildings, including Haggart's Stores on the left-hand corner.

Longstone village, looking east towards Slateford, showing Longstone Inn on the left. The chimneys of A. & J. Macnab's can be seen in the distance.

A class of 38 at the first Longstone School *c.* 1950.
Courtesy of Phyllis M. Cant (née Robson).

in and the ground grassed over but, in its heyday, provided employment for much of the male population of the village. It is known that Hailes Quarry was producing large quantities of stone around 1750 and that the workings grew to support a substantial industry before going into decline at the end of the nineteenth century. In 1892 George Craig made an interesting study of the sources of building stone used in Edinburgh. He describes Hailes as having been quarried to a depth of over a hundred feet in beds 'remarkable for the regularity of the laminae'. Three distinct colours of stone were produced: the lower levels produced a dark grey stone; the upper levels produced a red stone; and in various beds a blue tint was located. The hard, close-grained nature of the stone made it useful where great strength was required, notably in the construction of foundations. Its excellent resistance to weathering also made it a popular choice for many public and private buildings in Edinburgh: grey stone was used for Dalry School in 1876, Lochend Road School in 1886 and Sciennes School in 1891; blue stone was used for Plewlands Villa, Morningside, in 1878; and red stone for Red House, Cluny Gardens, in 1880.

Meantime, those readers who opted for the high-level view of Slateford and Longstone are still on the aqueduct! At present, the easiest way to get back to street level is to return to the timber steps at Prince Charlie's Bridge, but another flight of steps, linking the towpath directly to a new section of the Water of Leith Walkway, is currently proposed by the Water of Leith Conservation Trust as part of the Water of Leith Millennium Project. For those who are more energetic, there is the option of a circular walk of about a mile and a half, back to Slateford, by way of the canal towpath and the public pathway on the former railway track to Balerno. After heavy rainfall the going can be soft and occasionally the various paths are restricted by overhanging foliage.

From the west end of the aqueduct follow the towpath a few hundred yards with the railway on the right and Lanark Road on the far side of the canal. At the first stone bridge, which once carried the Balerno

George Bartie, the butcher, operated from very modest premises at the south-west end of Inglis Green Road in the 1920s and 1930s. He is seen here on his delivery rounds outside the Longstone Inn, which, at that time, was owned by the Murray family.

Another trader, specialising in home deliveries, was Liston & Brown, Fishmongers, who carried on business from No. 67 Slateford Road from c. 1917.

railway line across the canal, leave the towpath and go up the timber steps and cross the bridge beside the sign marked Stoneypath. Continue on a few paces to Easter Hailes Gate and take the pedestrian bridge over Lanark Road. The pedestrian bridge was erected some years ago to replace a much stronger, but shorter, railway bridge when Lanark Road was much narrower. The pathway is now on the old bed of the railway track and soon passes under a single-arch, ivy-covered stone bridge carrying Redhall Bank Road over the track bed. Further ahead there is a direction sign at the junction of four separate ways. The route, on which we have come, is signposted Slateford, and straight ahead is Balerno and Colinton Dell. Turn sharp left (no signpost) and take the partly cobbled path downhill with the Water of Leith coming in from the right. At the bottom of the hill is the site of Boag's Mill, long since demolished, beside a substantial stone bridge crossing the Water of Leith. This is a suitable point at which to consider some of the surrounding places of interest.

On the west bank is the site of Boag's Mill or Vernour's Mill dating from 1598 when it was a waulk mill. Its colourful history is described by John Geddie in equally colourful language:

The mossy bridge and white-washed group of houses at Boag's Mill occupy one of the prettiest and most secluded of the riverside nooks. The mill, one of the oldest on the Water, has shown marvellous power of adaptibility (sic). It has ground grain, and made paper and snuff. It turned out the first bank notes manufactured in Scotland, a picquet of soldiers mounting guard in the cottage on the bank above; and in the first decades of the century, when the Balfours were its tenants, the hospitable cellars of Boag's Mill entertained county magnates and bank directors. At present the dust-begrimed windows announce it to be still in part dedicated to meal and barley milling. But there comes wafted from the doors also a breath as from the spicy East. For along with the more commonplace output of peasemeal and pot barley – besides grinding chemicals, breaking sugar, and turning millwrights' machinery – the wheels of Boag's Mill liberate upon the air of the Water the pungent flavour of pepper, curry, and ginger, and the sweet odours of cinnamon, mace and cassia.

Redhall House, designed by James Robertson for George Inglis of Auchendinny in 1758, was unoccupied when this photograph was taken in 1986. The building has subsequently been restored. *Photograph by Graham C. Cant.*

The quotation is from *The Home Country of Robert Louis Stevenson* which Geddie wrote in 1898. Unfortunately, Boag's Mill was burned to the ground in 1924.

From the same vantage point (beside the stone bridge) it is possible to see, when the foliage is light, the outline of Redhall House high above the east bank. The house, recently saved from a short period of decline, is of great antiquity. The original approach was by the stone bridge at Boag's Mill. The lands of Redhall, or Reidhall, and the Castle belonged to Sir Adam Otterburn, King's Advocate from 1524 to 1538, and Lord Provost of Edinburgh on several occasions, namely 1522, 1528–1532, 1543–4 and 1547–8. Sir Adam was a man of varied talents who undertook several diplomatic journeys as ambassador to England and to France. He was in office as Lord Provost shortly after the defeat of the Scots at the Battle of Pinkie in 1547, and was assassinated by a servant of Governor Arran in the aftermath of the Earl of Hertford's invasions.

Redhall was purchased in 1755 by George Inglis of Auchendinny who commissioned James Robertson to design the present house in 1758. It was built as a five-bay block of two main storeys, attic and basement, with an advanced centre supporting a pediment, enhanced by three large urns. The substantial west wing and the ornate front porch with Ionic pillars and balustrades were added in 1900 when most of the interior was redesigned. The outside of the house is devoid of dates, initials or other inscriptions except for some roughly hewn stones set into the south-west corner which may have been intended for some ornamental addition.

Nothing remains at the site of the former Redhall Castle which lay approximately one hundred yards north-west of the present house. Around 1900 an excavation of the site revealed only the footing of a small semicircular turret approximately seven feet in diameter. However, an interesting panel depicting the arms of the Otterburn family was removed from the castle and built into the north side of the hexagonal doocot standing two hundred and fifty yards north-east of the house. It is believed that the doocot, the only one of its kind in Edinburgh, was built in 1756 by John Christy for the sum of forty pounds.

In 1945 A. Niven Robertson included Redhall in a most informative article entitled 'Old Dovecots in and around Edinburgh' for Volume

XXV of *The Book of the Old Edinburgh Club*. Each of the doocot's six walls is ten feet wide and two feet thick, constructed of red sandstone on a slightly projecting plinth. The walls are divided by a single stringcourse midway between the plinth and the eaves. On the south side, which contains the door, there is an empty square recess below the stringcourse, and a blocked-up window above it. The roof was slated, with the pigeon holes arranged in three rows, each with landing boards and four holes, and the apex carried a pole on which sat a nine-point star. At the present day the entire roof has been destroyed. The north wall was more elaborate than the south wall. Below the stringcourse a large semicircular recess, which may have been intended for a statue, has been blocked up. Above the stringcourse is the Otterburn coat of arms containing a shield with a chevron and three otters' heads, supported by two rampant wyverns with barbed tails intertwined, and parrot-like beaks. The Otterburn motto DE VIR- TUTE IN VIRTUTEM is carved below the shield. The inside of the doocot is now completely destroyed. Originally there were 757 nest holes in twenty tiers, all of which were made of wood except the two lowest tiers which were of stone. The stone nest holes were arranged in a circle but the wooden ones formed a dodecagon i.e. having twelve sides.

To the south-west of Redhall House, the stable block with the carved stone horse on the main gable dates from around 1758. Two modern special schools, Graysmill and Cairnpark, both built of yellow brick, were erected in the grounds in 1976.

From the stone bridge at Boag's Mill it is possible to reach Slateford by following the path, downstream, on either side of the Water of Leith. The west bank (without crossing the bridge) brings us closer to the places of interest. Take the path on the west bank and carry on past the allotments on the left-hand side until you reach a short flight of stone steps near the Water. Go down the steps and along the pathway towards Redhall Walled Garden, first laid out around 1756 by Robert Bowie, and still fully cultivated. The Walled Garden is the site of the former Lumsdaine's Mill which went under the intriguing name of Jinkaboot, probably taken from the unusual clattering sound of old mill machinery in motion. It is believed to have been operating as a corn mill in 1506, a paper mill in 1714, and a barley mill from 1735 to 1755, before being demolished and replaced by the walled kitchen garden for Redhall House.

At this point there is a short detour of a few hundred yards up the access road from the Walled Garden to Lanark Road. At the first bend, on the left, is an old cottage, recently renovated, which was originally designed by the architect, Sir James Gowans, in a similar style to, but much smaller than, Rockville which stood in Napier Road until recent years. The cottage is believed to date from 1863 when it was probably used by the quarrymaster at nearby Redhall Quarry which had been leased to Gowans' father. Originally, the accommodation was a modest single-storey structure in the shape of a crucifix, with a central chimney serving two open fireplaces. Unfortunately no evidence remains of exactly how the internal space was divided. Externally, the stonework was typically the work of Gowans, the modular banding being empha-sised by different coloured stone. Sometime after the Second World War, two brick and harled extensions were built – but not in keeping with Gowans' design: a kitchen was built to the north-west and a bedroom, toilet and store were built to the south-west. The cottage became progressively run-down from the mid-1970s, but after it came into private hands in 1996 it was given a new lease of life. The roof was reconstructed, the external stonework was repaired and modern services were installed. The post-war brick extensions were demolished and replaced by new extensions more in keeping with the architectural importance of the original design. Part of the interior has been given a split-level floor and the extensions include two bedrooms and a conservatory. The completed work has, undoubtedly, saved a small architectural gem, by one of Scotland's leading architects, from almost certain dereliction.

The cottage is only a short distance from Lanark Road but to continue the walk we retrace our steps to the Walled Garden and cross the narrow timber pedestrian bridge (halfway along the east wall) to the other side of the Water of Leith. We are now on the last leg of the walk, past the stone gazebo, on the right, by Robert Bowie who also laid out the Walled Garden. Within a few hundred yards the dell suddenly opens out at the Tickled Trout on Lanark Road. The low Tudor-style building, recently occupied by a veterinary surgeon, was the original north lodge to Craiglockhart House.

On the far side of Lanark Road is the former Slateford School which we saw from the canal aqueduct at the start of the walk. Since 1989 the building has been the headquarters of the Water of Leith Conservation Trust, formed in 1988 with the object of 'involving the local community in the conservation of the Water of Leith as an amenity, wildlife and educational resource'. Following a successful bid for finance to the Millennium Commission, substantial upgrading of the building was agreed in 1998. Prior to that, all the available accommodation was on one floor which included an office and a large hall used for lectures and a permanent display of material relating to the work of the Trust. The new plans, drawn by the architect, Malcolm Fraser, include a new entrance, foyer, shop, library, exhibition area, teaching room, meeting room and utilities, all on the ground floor. A new staircase gives access to an office built into the extended attic space of the old building. The new Centre is the focal point for the Water of Leith, 'providing a unique and exciting range of exhibits exploring all aspects of the river'. It is open to the public and provides an educational service to schools and other interested groups.

A further section of the Water of Leith Walkway is also envisaged which will connect two existing parts of the Walkway. The new section will begin at the Trust headquarters and run north-east towards the

Records for Slateford School are available from 1864 but it is clear that a school existed prior to that date on the same site. In 1999 the building was extended and renovated as the headquarters of the Water of Leith Conservation Trust. Photographed in 1986.

aqueduct where the path will be carried on a platform cantilevered out from the side of one of the aqueduct supports. A similar arrangement will be made to bypass the railway viaduct. From there, the new Walkway will continue on the east bank, skirting Saughton Cemetery and the allotments, and cross a new pedestrian bridge near the south end of Stenhouse Mill Lane. The last section will be constructed on the west bank of the Water to Gorgie Road to join up with the existing walkway across Gorgie Road and downstream to Balgreen.

Our walk finishes at Prince Charlie's Bridge which displays the year of construction, 1937, on its west parapet. The wide, single, reinforced-concrete span replaced a much shorter stone bridge constructed when the canal was first opened. Below the north side of the new bridge is a small bronze plaque commemorating a much earlier event:

Prince Charlie Bridge
Near this spot at Gray's Mill
Prince Charlie's Army Halted
in 1745 prior to the occupation
of Edinburgh

Before leaving Longstone and Slateford it is interesting to consider some of the problems encountered when the Union Canal was first proposed.

THE UNION CANAL

Towards the end of the eighteenth century several speculative reports were compiled on the possibility of linking Edinburgh and Glasgow by a ship canal suitable for freight and passenger services. At a meeting of interested parties in Edinburgh in January 1793, John Ainslie and Robert Whitworth were appointed to make the necessary survey. Four separate routes were suggested, to which John Rennie, the bridge engineer, added a fifth, to the north of the others. Some years later, amid growing doubts about the commercial viability of the scheme, Hugh Baird was commissioned to draw up another report with the assistance of Francis Hall, the surveyor. The result was a lengthy *Report on the Proposed Edinburgh and Glasgow Union Canal* dated 20th September 1813 in which Baird explained the line of the canal, the technical difficulties, the anticipated objections and, most importantly, the estimated costs and expected revenues.

The children of Colinton Sunday School leave Stoneyport on the Union Canal (near Lanark Road) for their annual picnic to Ratho. *Courtesy of the late Miss E. D. Robertson.*

Baird proposed a contour canal, without locks, from Lothian Road in Edinburgh to join the Forth and Clyde Canal at Falkirk, a distance of twenty-eight miles, being only four miles more than the turnpike road. To accommodate boats up to thirty tons the canal had to be five feet deep, twenty feet wide at the bottom, and thirty-five feet wide at the surface of the water. The problem of providing that amount of water constantly was more difficult than the layman might imagine. Canals leak. They also lose millions of gallons of water by absorption, evaporation and the effects of the wind. Baird also faced a daily loss of water through the lock system linking the Union Canal with the existing Forth and Clyde Canal. He calculated that the canal would need to be replenished to the extent of seventy-two million cubic feet of water every year. That figure would be required for four months of the year only as it was anticipated that for the greater part of the year

Although the original aqueduct eventually created a serious traffic obstruction, its massive stone supports provided ample space for the advertisements of the day: Chivers Jellies; Raleigh Bicycles; Scott's Porage Oats; and Zebo: 'so clean, so quick, so bright'. The bridge was replaced by the present reinforced-concrete structure in 1937.
Courtesy of Edinburgh City Libraries.

the canal could be topped up by the numerous rivers and burns along its route. Substantial reservoirs were proposed to deal with the summer months when it was anticipated that complaints would be received from the mill owners who relied on the water of the River Almond to power their machinery. The total cost of the canal, basins, aqueducts and reservoirs was estimated at £235,167. Baird also outlined the economic reasons for building the canal. One of the main arguments was that great savings had been made by utilising the Forth and Clyde Canal instead of taking a direct route to Glasgow. He also produced compelling figures on the uneconomic cost of road transport between the two main cities in Scotland, and detailed the various commodities which would be conveyed much more cheaply by water. Baird's report was considered at a General Meeting of Subscribers at the Town Hall of Linlithgow on 8th October 1813, but the following year the Magistrates of Edinburgh objected to the plans and appointed Robert Stevenson (grandfather of Robert Louis Stevenson) to advise on a

different route to connect with Leith Docks. Bitter controversy followed, with allegations that Baird's plan favoured his own coalmining
interests to the west of Edinburgh. By 1817, however, the Union Canal
Act was passed and Baird was instructed to begin work. On Tuesday
3rd March 1818, after the adjournment of a General Meeting, the
Committee of Management proceeded to the west end of Fountain-
bridge 'attended by a vast number of people to witness the
commencement of so grand an improvement to the Metropolis'. A
prayer was said by the Rev. David Dickson, and Mr Downie of Appin,
Chairman of the Committee of Management, dug the first spadeful,
proclaiming that the entire venture would bring much-needed employment to the city. By 1822 the first passenger boats, *Flora MacIvor* and
Di Vernon, were in operation and the canal was opened in May 1823,
by which time the estimated cost of £235,167 in 1813 had risen to an
actual cost of £461,760.

An undertaking of that magnitude is seldom accomplished without
difficulties and alterations to the original plan. One such alteration at
the Edinburgh end of the works is of particular interest. Baird proposed

Looking north-west across the green of Slateford Bowling Club in 1986. The
aqueduct, carrying the Union Canal, is nearer to the camera, with the smaller
arches of the railway viaduct behind.

that a branch of the canal be built at Gilmore Place to enter the Meadows through Mr Haig's Lochrin Distillery at the junction of present-day Home Street and Gilmore Place. As the canal would have crossed 'the Linton Road', a drawbridge with a house and keeper was proposed. After passing by the north end of Drumdryen House the canal entered the Meadows, crossed the Middle Meadow Walk about fifty yards below the North Walk and passed the Archers' Butts to a basin at the east end of the Meadows. Where the canal ran through the Meadows it was to be faced in stone on the north side for taking up and landing passengers. The total cost of £8,203 was considered to be too costly and Baird was instructed by the Subscribers to abandon that section of the works. In addition, at Slateford, Baird's original idea for a four-arch aqueduct was replaced by an eight-arch aqueduct, six hundred feet long and sixty feet high. The bed of the canal on the aqueduct was lined with iron and iron balustrades were erected on each side. Altogether it was a magnificent feat of engineering described by Telford as 'superior perhaps to any aqueduct in the Kingdom'.

Dark days lay ahead. Ten years were spent planning and building the Union Canal. Almost twenty years after *Flora MacIvor* sailed out of Port Hopetoun (later occupied by Lothian House in Lothian Road) with a cargo of excited passengers, the Edinburgh and Glasgow Railway Company opened a line from Edinburgh to Glasgow. Passengers travelling by boat ceased immediately and in 1849 the Railway Company bought the canal for £209,000 – less than half the cost of its construction. Despite the early decline of passenger traffic, freight was carried on the Union Canal for most of the twentieth century. The present owners are the British Waterways.

Today the Union Canal enjoys a revival as a place of leisure and recreational interests, rather than its original function as a commercial waterway. Its tunnels, aqueducts, bridges and embankments remain as important examples of industrial archaeology and Ancient Monuments. It is planned to reopen the Union Canal to navigation, including the section at Wester Hailes in Edinburgh which was put underground in the 1960s. This work will form part of a much grander Millennium Link to re-establish navigation along the Union Canal and the Forth and Clyde Canal 'City to City and Coast to Coast'. Boats will be raised and lowered twenty-five metres by a giant 'wheel' between the levels of the two canals at Falkirk.

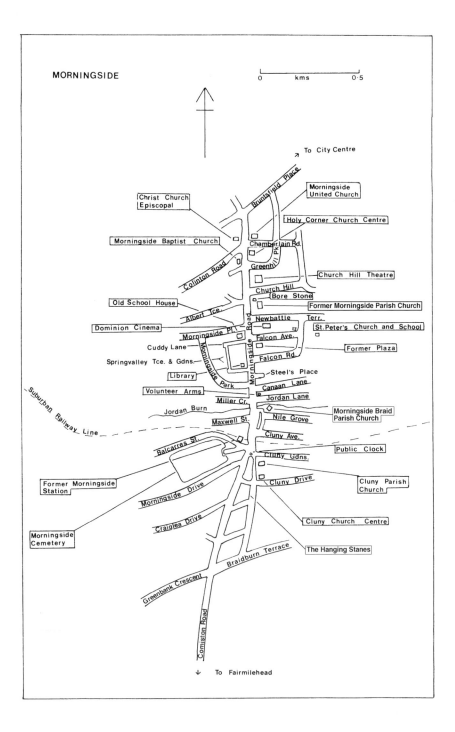

MORNINGSIDE

0 kms 0·5

To City Centre

Bruntsfield Place

Morningside
United Church

Christ Church
Episcopal

Holy Corner Church Centre

Morningside Baptist Church

Chamberlain Rd.

Greenhill Pl.

Colinton Road

Church Hill Theatre

Church Hill

Bore Stone

Old School House

Former Morningside Parish Church

Albert Tce.

Dominion Cinema

Newbattle Terr.

St. Peter's Church and School

Morningside Pl.

Falcon Ave.

Cuddy Lane

Morningside Road

Falcon Rd.

Former Plaza

Springvalley Tce. & Gdns.

Morningside Park

Steel's Place

Library

Canaan Lane

Volunteer Arms

Jordan Lane

Miller Cr.

Suburban Railway Line

Jordan Burn

Nile Grove

Morningside Braid
Parish Church

Maxwell St.

Cluny Ave.

Public Clock

Balcarres St.

Cluny Gdns.

Former Morningside
Station

Cluny Drive

Cluny Parish
Church

Morningside Drive

Cluny Church Centre

Craiglea Drive

Morningside
Cemetery

The Hanging Stanes

Braidburn Terrace

Greenbank Crescent

Comiston Road

↓ To Fairmilehead

CHAPTER SIX

Morningside

Morningside, as the name may infer, lies on a south-sloping aspect to the south of Church Hill, on the old road from Tollcross to Biggar. Its origins are undoubtedly agricultural, when it served as a centre of population to the many neighbouring farms and estates, Plewlands, the Grange of St Giles, Oxgangs, Braid, Greenbank and Comiston, and the biblically-named Canaan and Egypt. One of the earliest maps to show Morningside is Richard Cooper's *Plan of the City of Edinburgh and Adjacent Grounds*, in 1759, on which the village is represented by only a handful of houses. By the 1880s Grant, in *Old and New Edinburgh*, was able to say that Morningside was 'once a secluded village, consisting of little more than a row of thatched cottages, a line of trees, and a blacksmith's forge, from which it gradually grew to become an agreeable environ and summer resort of the citizens, with the fame of being the "Montpellier" of the east of Scotland, alluring invalids to its precincts for the benefit of its mild salubrious air'. A century later, whilst the climate may not have altered very much, the appearance of Morningside Road has altered completely from that of the main street of a quiet country village. Although the transformation from village to suburb was gradual, at least two factors combined to precipitate the change: in 1885 the Edinburgh Suburban and South Side Junction Railway was opened with a goods yard at the west end of Maxwell Street; and simultaneously a proliferation of villas and mansions was increasing the population dramatically. Around the same time, many of the old cottages which had lined each side of the main street were demolished for the construction of four-storey tenement buildings which completely dwarfed the remaining houses. The main part of the village lay to the west of Morningside Road between the Old Schoolhouse and what is now Morningside Park.

The story of Morningside and its fascinating anecdotes, characters and buildings is related with great panache by its local author and historian, Charles J. Smith, in *Historic South Edinburgh*. Towards the end of his account of Morningside, Mr Smith concludes that 'In the chronological sequence of smiddy, inn, village school and Parish Church can be traced the development of the community'.

Morningside United Church at Chamberlain Road, Holy Corner, in which the congregation is both part of the Church of Scotland and of the Congregational Union of Scotland. The spire of Christ Church Episcopal is on the left of the picture. *Photograph by Phyllis M. Cant.*

HOLY CORNER TO BRAID ROAD

No study of the route between Holy Corner and Braid Road would be complete without mentioning the many churches which have been established over the years. The story of their evolution and involvement in the community, through periods of unity and disunity, presents an interesting microcosm of church history. At Holy Corner there are four main church buildings.

Christ Church Episcopal, on the north corner of Colinton Road and Morningside Road, was designed in the French-Gothic style by the famous architect Hippolyte J. Blanc, who was also a member of the congregation. The builders were W. & J. Kirkwood who had completed only part of the work by the time the church was opened on 4th June 1876. Work on the chancel, tower and spire was completed later by a gift from Miss Falconar of Falcon Hall, in memory of her father, a founder member of Morningside Parish Church. The church was dedicated by Bishop Cotterill on 12th March 1878.

A less grand building was erected on the north corner of Morningside Road and Chamberlain Road in 1863 for Morningside United Presbyterian congregation. When the building became too small for the increased congregation, a new church was built on the south corner, and was opened in 1881 as North Morningside United Presbyterian Church. For a time, their old building on the north corner was used by the Morningside Athenaeum Club which provided a library, lecture theatre and concert hall for its members. The Athenaeum was bought by Morningside Congregational Church in 1890 and used as their place of worship until 1927 when it was demolished and replaced by the present building, designed by James McLachlan with an attractive small-scale campanile. In 1980 North Morningside Church and Morningside Congregational Church joined to form Morningside United Church, a unique union in which the congregation is both part of the Church of Scotland and part of the Congregational Union of Scotland. The former North Morningside Church building (on the south corner) is now the home of the Eric Liddell Centre, administered by a Board of Directors from a membership originated by members of Morningside United Church, Christ Church and Morningside Baptist Church. The Centre takes its name from Eric Liddell, the Olympic runner and missionary known to the world through the film *Chariots of Fire*, who

The former North Morningside Church, at Holy Corner, is now used as the Eric Liddell Centre. *Photograph by Phyllis M. Cant.*

was a member of Morningside Congregational Church. Work on the Centre was started several years ago and has now reached the stage where the ground floor of the old church building houses the Sycomore Coffee House and Bookshop, and other halls. These are used for a variety of community care and community education projects, including the Chinese Evangelical Church, the Napier Club, the Outlook Club and many others. The eventual aim, on which agreement has been reached, is to convert the internal space into five separate levels.

Before progressing southwards on Morningside Road, a short detour along Chamberlain Road provides the opportunity to visit the burial place of John Livingston of Greenhill. The tomb is located in a small enclosure on the north side of Chamberlain Road, immediately west of the junction with Greenhill Gardens. John Livingston owned the estate of Greenhill when he died of the plague in 1645 at the age of 53.

Christ Church Episcopal, at Holy Corner, on the north corner of Colinton
Road and Morningside Road, designed in 1875 by Hippolyte J. Blanc.
Photograph by Phyllis M. Cant.

Morningside Baptist Church, at Holy Corner, was formed in 1894 in the building originally designed by MacGibbon & Ross in 1872 for the Free Church. *Photograph by Graham C. Cant.*

The tombstone, which is still fairly legible, bears the motto 'MORS PATET: HORA LATET' (death is certain: the hour unknown), the initials I.L. for John Livingston, and a long inscription in memory of the deceased. The tomb, and the area of ground around it, has recently been renovated by the City following representations from the Greenhill and Church Hill Amenity Association.

Back on Morningside Road, Morningside Baptist Church lies on the west side almost opposite the junction with Greenhill Park. Immediately to the south of the church, a short lane leads to Masonic Hall Abbotsford. The present building was developed from a much earlier house, Grangebank Cottage, home of John George Bartholomew until his death in 1861. The building, which is currently under redevelopment, represents the last remnant of the old village of Boroughmuirhead. Morningside Baptist Church was opened in 1894 with a very small congregation, following a meeting of interested parties in Torrance's Tea Room on the south corner of Belhaven Terrace. The building, designed by MacGibbon & Ross in 1872, was previously used by the Free Church who sold it to the Baptists and moved a short distance, south, to a new red sandstone church, designed by Hippolyte J. Blanc. This church was later designated Morningside High Church which amalgamated with Morningside Parish Church in 1960. Thereafter, the building, previously used by Morningside High Church, became the Church Hill Theatre. In the forecourt of the theatre, two ornamental pillars, known as the Church Hill Milestones, were erected in 1996. They were commissioned by the Church Hill Theatre Public Art Group in partnership with Edinburgh District Council and several amenity associations. The design, by Kenny Munro, includes the district names Greenhill, Merchiston, Boroughmuir, Church Hill, Morningside and Tipperlinn, along with various insets depicting aspects of the district, for example, the Bore Stone, a Shuttle for the weavers of Tipperlinn, and a Piano and Kipper, reinforcing the 'music hall' adage about Morningside.

It is not easy to imagine present-day Morningside Road as the main street through a quiet rural village. However, there remain a sufficient number of buildings to provide some idea of the basic layout. In 1586 the Burgh Muir was divided into four lots, one of which was Morningside Estate, consisting of twenty-six acres to the west of what is now Morningside Road. It was bounded on the north by Albert Terrace,

John M. Comrie and his daughter, Betty, outside the family business on the
north corner of Colinton Road and Morningside Road in 1957. The nursery
and florists were first taken over by John M. Comrie in 1928 and later
became Mulhearn & Brotchie.
Courtesy of Mrs Betty Cunningham, née Comrie.

on the south by the Jordan Burn, and on the west by Myreside. Within
this large tract of land there were three separate villages, Morningside,
Myreside and Tipperlinn, of which only Morningside has survived. On
the east side of the road through Morningside lay the lands of Canaan,
delineated in an interesting *Plan of Canaan*, dated 1802, now in Register
House. The plan, surveyed by Thomas Johnston, was probably drawn
up during a lawsuit between William Mossman of Canaan and Major
Archibald Mossman. It shows the lands of Canaan divided into twenty-
two lots, mainly of three acres each, bounded on the north by the Road
to Grange, now Newbattle Terrace; on the south by the Burn of Jordan
and the Lands of Braid; on the west by the road from Edinburgh to
Biggar, now Morningside Road; and on the east by the Lands of

Blackford. The original feuars included several names which constantly reappear in the early history of Morningside: Alex Adie, James Belfrage, William Coulter and John Ross, followed later by Lady Oswald and the Falconar family.

Although the first *Ordnance Survey Map* of 1852 clearly shows the line of Morningside Road, it was not until 1885 that its designation and house numbering were applied continuously from Holy Corner to Morningside Road Station. Prior to that, Morningside Road consisted of a series of short sections, each of which had its own name. On the west side, starting at Holy Corner and going south, the names, at varying dates, were: Waverley Terrace (Baptist Church to Church Hill); Marmion Terrace (Church Hill to Abbotsford Park); Morningside Bank (Abbotsford Park to Morningside Place); Esplin Place and Blackford Place (Cuddy Lane to Springvalley Gardens); and Watt Terrace (Maxwell Street to Morningside Station). On the east side, also starting at Holy Corner and going south, again at varying dates, the names were: Greenhill Bank (Holy Corner to Church Hill Place); Banner Place (Church Hill Place to Newbattle Terrace); Falcon Place (Newbattle Terrace to Falcon Road West); Morningside Terrace (Falcon Road West to Canaan Lane); and Jordan Place (Canaan Lane to Jordan Lane).

As we proceed southwards, down Morningside Road, the first point of interest, on the left, is the so-called Bore Stone. It sits high above the pavement, accompanied by a large bronze plaque on which it is claimed that it is the stone 'In which the Royal Standard was last pitched for the muster of the Scottish Army on the Borough Muir before the Battle of Flodden 1513'. Romantic and stirring as the inscription might be, the authenticity of the stone is seriously challenged in a very scholarly article by Henry M. Paton, published in 1942, in Vol. XXIV of *The Book of the Old Edinburgh Club*. In more recent times, Stuart Harris in *The Place Names of Edinburgh* says that the Bore Stone, or Hare Stane as he prefers to call it, was probably a marker stone for the surrounding estates. He gives no credence at all to the popularly held belief that the stone once held the Royal Standard.

On the other side of the road, a smaller stone offers considerably less scope for historical debate, with the inscription:

ONE MILE FROM TOLLCROSS

On the wall of the former Morningside Parish Church is the Bore Stone, said to have held the Royal Standard for the muster of the Scottish Army on the Burgh Muir before the Battle of Flodden, 1513. *Photograph by Phyllis M. Cant.*

To the south of the Bore Stone, or Hare Stane, is the former Morningside Parish Church, opened on 29th July 1838 following a very successful appeal for funds during the previous year. A long list of subscribers, headed by Alexander Falconar of Falcon Hall and his five daughters, pledged over £2,000 – well in excess of the estimated cost of £1,600. The architect, John Henderson, provided plans for 634 sittings, including a front gallery, with provision for two side galleries when required, and the plot of land was gifted by Sir John Stuart Forbes, proprietor of the lands of Greenhill. The church bell was provided from Whitechapel Foundry but Mr Henderson's drawings did not allow for a clock within the slender spire. In 1840 the congregation bought the mechanism of the clock from the Old Schoolhouse across the road, and transferred it to the church. It remained there until 1929,

Morningside Parish Church, on the corner of Newbattle Terrace and Morningside Road, was opened on 29th July 1838. After the congregation united with Braid Church in 1990 to form Morningside Braid Parish Church, the former Parish Church building was sold to Napier University.

by which time it was probably more than a century old, and was replaced at a cost of £64. In 1868 the church was enlarged by the addition of an apse to the east, and transepts to the north and south, designed by Peddie & Kinnear. The 1868 apse was replaced in 1888 by a chancel designed by Hardy & Wight. Sadly Morningside Parish

Church was closed for worship in 1990 when the congregation amalgamated with Braid Church. The old Morningside Parish Church building was sold to Napier University and Braid Church became the home of the combined congregations, under the designation Morningside Braid Parish Church.

Most of the old village of Morningside lay on the west side of the main road, between Cuddy Lane and Morningside Park. Cuddy Lane, formerly known as Rosewood Lane, led to Springvalley House, a fine old mansion set in its own grounds, once the home of James Grant, author of *Old and New Edinburgh*, among other works. The house was demolished in 1907 but is commemorated by a stone plaque set into the tenement of Nos. 43 and 45 Springvalley Terrace. In Cuddy Lane two buildings date from at least 1823. Rosewood Cottage (now No. 6 Cuddy Lane) was built for Miss Ann Henderson but was divided into two dwellings around 1944, the east section retaining the name Rosewood Cottage and the west section being named The Cottage. In the back garden of The Cottage (No. 4), and also in a nearby house in Morningside Place, there are deep wells of fresh spring water, providing a tantalising clue to the significance of the name Springvalley. Immediately to the west of The Cottage is a larger two-storey building, Viewhill Cottage (now No. 2) , dating from the same period as Rosewood Cottage. From about 1900 to 1920 Viewhill Cottage was occupied by Austin's Family Laundry, first established in 1890 at No. 4 Jordan Lane. The tenement building immediately to the south of Cuddy Lane was built on an open piece of ground beside a short row of two-storey shops and houses. These formed part of the old village, along with another group to the rear. The forecourt of the Merlin bistro bar was the site of Dick Wright's smiddy, a plain two-storey building which closed around 1900. Afterwards it was occupied by a sculptor and tombstone maker on the ground floor. The upper storey was formerly the Blackford Press which took its name from the short section of Morningside Road in front of the Merlin, previously known as Blackford Place. The two-storey building and the sculptor's yard were removed when the Merlin was built.

One of the most significant buildings to survive from the old village is, of course, the Old Schoolhouse dating from 1823. It lies on the west side of Morningside Road to the north of Cuddy Lane. Four eminent citizens were closely involved in its formation: George Ross

The Old Schoolhouse, Morningside Road, dating from 1823, served the village population until 1892 when South Morningside School was opened. Since 1906 the Old Schoolhouse has been used by the Christian Brethren. *Courtesy of A. W. Brotchie.*

of Woodburn House; Alexander Falconar of Falcon Hall; James Evans of Canaan Park; and Henry Hare of Newgrange. It was George Ross, the distinguished judge, whose interest and financial backing ensured the continuation of the school, which became known as the Ross School. Although little is known of the masters and assistants when the school first opened, one name has survived several generations. Until recently there were a few senior citizens who could recall the most famous of all the village schoolmasters, Andrew Myrtle Cockburn, known to pupils and parents alike (though perhaps not in his presence) as 'Cocky' Cockburn. He came to the village school in 1873 from Redding, near Polmont, and transferred to South Morningside School as First Assistant when it opened in 1892. After the Old Schoolhouse was closed, the building was let, in 1906, by the owner, Peter Cowieson, to the Christian Brethren as a place of worship. In 1946 the building was sold to the Brethren subject to the express condition 'that it would continue as a place of Christian witness in the locality'. For many years this small church has been a centre of evangelical activity, with particular emphasis on concern for children. Immediately after the Second World War the Sunday School had more than one hundred children on the roll, most of whom came from families living in the neighbouring streets of Springvalley. Whilst that high level of attendance at Sunday School has not been maintained in recent years, there is, instead, greater emphasis on children's clubs and other activities during the week. Many members of the congregation have dedicated their lives to overseas mission service in different parts of the world, particularly in Zaire, formerly the Belgian Congo. In 1980 the fairly modest accommodation at Morningside Road was greatly improved by the addition of small single-storey wings to the north and south. The clock mechanism was also completely overhauled, ending a long period during which the hands were stuck at 3.40!

The old village extended southwards towards Morningside Park. Morningside Public Library, opened on 9th November 1904 by John Harrison, the second son of Lord Provost George Harrison, was built of Blackpastures stone from Northumberland on the site of Denholm's Smiddy and cottage. Adjacent to Denholm's Smiddy, at the north corner of Springvalley Gardens and Morningside Road, was the Free Church of Scotland School, the site now occupied by Nos. 190–196 Morningside Road. To the south of the Free Church School was Reid Lane leading to Reid's Cottages and a dairy farm owned for many years by John Reid. The cottages still exist, but the byres were demolished in 1899 for the construction of Springvalley Gardens and Terrace. The building to the west of the cottages housed Morningside's first cinema, opened prior to the First World War in what was then called Morningside Hall. The cinema continued until 1938 during which time it had several names, including Morningside Photoplay House, the Ritz Kinema, Evans Picture House, Cine Playhouse and finally Springvalley Cinema. Between 1914 and 1938 it had three owners, R. M. Ireland in 1914, followed by Thomas Butt, and then George Murray in the last few years of its existence. In the late 1930s the proprietors decided to close the cinema, perhaps on account of the opening of its main competitor, the Dominion, discussed later in this chapter. For a short while, the Springvalley Cinema became a dance hall under the name, the Del Mar, which was

(a) Thomas Chalmers, leader of the Disruption in 1843, lived at No. 1 Church Hill where Free Church services were held. *Photograph from Disruption Worthies.*

(b) Andrew Myrtle Cockburn ('Cocky' Cockburn), one-time 'maister' of the Old Schoolhouse. *Courtesy of his daughter, the late Mrs M. Wilson, and Charles Skilton Ltd.*

(c) Eric Liddell, the athlete and missionary, known to the world through the film *Chariots of Fire*. His name is remembered in the Eric Liddell Centre at Holy Corner. *Courtesy of* The Scotsman Publications Ltd.

(d) Charles J. Smith, lecturer and author of *Historic South Edinburgh* and other works, a lifelong resident of Morningside. *Photograph by C. P. Smith.*

acquired by one of Edinburgh's early exhibition organisers, David Sharp, who reopened the ballroom in September 1938 as the Silver Slipper. On the opening night 250 couples danced the night away to the music of Symon Stungo and his band, 'accompanied' by several canaries in a huge barrel-shaped cage. For couples taking a leisurely seat there was the added attraction of 'tables which contained tanks with goldfish, covered with plate-glass tops'. Morningside's other dance halls included the Abbotsford Dance Hall at Masonic Lodge Abbotsford, near Holy Corner, and the Dunedin Dance Hall at Masonic Lodge Dunedin in Morningside Drive. The Plaza is discussed later in this chapter.

One of the principal mansions of the district was Morningside House which stood in its own grounds, set back from Morningside Road on land now occupied by a supermarket on the north corner of Morningside Park and Morningside Road. It is difficult to date Morningside House because some reports confuse it with the much grander Falcon Hall, or Morningside Lodge, to the east. The best-informed opinion is that Morningside House was probably built around 1780 for Lord Gardenstone, the somewhat eccentric Senator of the College of Justice who came to live in Morningside in 1789. Kay's *Original Portraits* portrays Lord Gardenstone, 'distinguished as a man of some talent and much eccentricity', riding into town on horseback with a young boy in Highland dress running behind. The boy was employed to look after the horse during the time that the court was in session, and then to run all the way back to Morningside in the evening. The judge's affection for animals was not confined to horses. Even if the law was not an ass, at least it was close to a pig! Before retiring to bed in the winter, his lordship allowed one of his favourite pigs to sleep in his bed to warm it up, and then to spend the rest of the night lying on his clothes to make them warm and comfortable for the morning. Lord Gardenstone's pig has not forsaken Morningside. It appears in a most interesting composition, entitled 'Painting of Tenements', by Margaret S. White which hangs in Morningside Library. The scene shows the pig at a tenement window, above 'the T.S.B.', looking out over the streets of Springvalley which bustle with everyday activities over the years, including a wedding, children playing and couples dancing in the street. The painting was commissioned by Morningside Community Council in 1992 to commemorate the life of Anna Tocher, Community Councillor and Historian, who grew up in Morningside.

Later in life Lord Gardenstone was deeply involved in improving the living conditions of the inhabitants of Laurencekirk near his estate of Johnstone, and in the erection of St Bernard's Well at Stockbridge. After he died in 1793 Morningside House and estate passed to his nephew who sold it to David Deuchar, the distinguished etcher and engraver. The Deuchar family remained there until the early 1870s after which Morningside House was occupied by John Reid, the dairyman, until it was demolished in 1895. The tenement which stands on the site contains a sculptured panel commemorating the Diamond Jubilee of Queen Victoria in 1897.

The lands of Canaan lay to the east side of Morningside Road, marked by a long line of old cottages which were demolished during the tenement-building era of the late nineteenth century. In the early part of the nineteenth century Alexander Falconar built Falcon Hall on the Canaan estate, possibly incorporating an earlier house known as Morningside Lodge. When completed, Falcon Hall was a very grand building of two principal storeys, with a façade of twelve monolithic pillars. Four pillars created an imposing entrance above which were eight pillars, in pairs, supporting a broad pediment. On the ground floor the pillars were flanked by statues of Nelson and Wellington. Despite their apparently opulent lifestyle, the Falconars were generous benefactors to the local community and in particular to Morningside Parish Church and Christ Church Episcopal. After the last of the five Falconar daughters died in 1887, Falcon Hall became a boarding school for boys under the name Morningside College. The College was established in Morningside Drive in 1882; it transferred to Rockville House in Napier Road in 1889; and in 1890 it set up in Falcon Hall for only a few years. All the resident masters were graduates of Oxford or Cambridge, the 1888 report saying that 'the very competent and ample staff are evidently enthusiasts in the cause of education and earnestly devoted to their duties in their several departments'.

According to *Plans and Notes of the Landed Estates of the Merchant Company Institutions*, 1891, eighteen acres of land between Church Lane (Newbattle Terrace) and Canaan Lane were purchased by George Watson's Hospital from the Trustees of the Misses Falconar and Mrs Craigie of Falcon Hall in 1889 for £33,000. Strips of ground were also sold to the City for £1,195 to widen Newbattle Terrace and Morningside Road. Reference to the Minute Books of George Watson's Hospital for 1894 and 1895 suggests that the Governors were beginning to consider some form of development of the house and grounds. On 13th December 1894 they adopted a suggestion of the architects MacGibbon & Ross that the entrance gates and pillars should be advertised for sale by private bargain, and that the purchaser was to remove the material at his own expense. A few weeks later, on 3rd January 1895, the Committee authorised the sale of the gates and pillars to John White, the builder, of No. 79 Craiglea Drive, for £25. The Minutes do not record whether Mr White proceeded with the job immediately but it was not until December 1906 that the Governors asked if the occupier of Falcon Hall, John George Bartholomew, wished to renew the lease which was due to expire at Whitsunday 1907. Mr Bartholomew confirmed on 14th March 1907 that he would not be renewing and, after several abortive proposals, the builder J. M. Cruikshank suggested in July 1907 that the mansion should be demolished. The Committee agreed, subject to ten items of historical interest being preserved, which included the statues of Wellington and Nelson, several falcons, marble door-jambs and tinted glass from the circular room. On 10th August 1907 Mr Birnie Rhind R.S.A. compiled a report on the statues which were to be presented to the City 'for the Art Gallery or the front of a new Art School', but this idea was never implemented. Fortunately, when Falcon Hall was eventually demolished in 1909 the pillared façade, and the balustrade of the staircase and balcony, were removed at the instigation of John George Bartholomew and rebuilt at the headquarters of Bartholomews, the cartographers, in Duncan Street. The gates and pillars with the falcons, for which Mr White agreed to pay £25, now stand at the entrance to Edinburgh Zoo at Corstorphine.

The gradual demise of Falcon Hall paved the way for further development of the area to the east of Morningside Road. Several streets of tenement buildings were constructed as well as St Peter's Roman Catholic Church in 1906, and the School in 1909. St Peter's Church was the brainchild of two men, John Gray and André Raffalovitch, whose paths had crossed in the literary circles of London in the late 1880s. Gray resigned from his position as librarian to the Foreign Office to enter the priesthood in 1901, and was appointed curate at St Patrick's Church in the Cowgate in Edinburgh. His friendship with Raffalovitch continued and was greatly strengthened in 1905 when Raffalovitch moved to Edinburgh and took up residence at No. 9 Whitehouse

St Peter's Roman Catholic Church in Falcon Avenue was designed in 1905 by
Sir Robert Lorimer, and opened on 25th April 1907.

Terrace. In that same year the two men resolved to build a new Roman
Catholic church in Morningside, mainly from a generous donation by
Raffalovitch. The site on the north corner of Falcon Avenue and Falcon
Gardens was purchased from the Merchant Company in May 1905,
and Sir Robert Lorimer was commissioned to draw the plans for what
turned out to be one of his greatest achievements. The foundation stone
was laid on 17th April 1906 by Archbishop James Augustine Smith. A
few years later, in 1909 the Archbishop also laid the foundation stone
for St Peter's School, which was opened in Falcon Gardens, nearby, on
4th April 1910. Father (later Canon) John Gray of St Peter's Church
was appointed as the school manager, and Sister Agnes McMullen, a
Sister of Charity, acted as head teacher. The management of the school
was transferred from the Church to the Education Authority in 1919,
and in 1966 the administration of St Ignatius Primary School at Glen
Street and Chalmers Street was incorporated into St Peter's.

Tommy Meek, on the left, and Mike Imrie, on the right, doormen at the Plaza Ballroom in 1933. The Plaza opened in 1926 and closed in 1975, the site now being occupied by a Safeway Store. *From* Oh, How We Danced! *Courtesy of Elizabeth Casciani.*

In the world of entertainment, Morningside attracted two 'institutions' which became synonymous with the district, firstly the Plaza Ballroom in 1926, and then the Dominion Cinema in 1938. The story of the Plaza has been expertly researched by Elizabeth Casciani in her history of ballroom dancing in Scotland, *Oh, How We Danced!* The founder of the Plaza, Charles Jones, started in the motor business in Peebles but later moved to Edinburgh where he set up a garage in Lothian Road, before coming to Morningside. He acquired the site on the corner of Falcon Avenue and Morningside Road for Jones Motor House, a spacious complex to include workshops, service areas, filling station, showroom and public hall. It was this latter accommodation which proved to be a tentative step in the right direction, as reported in the *Motor Trader and Review* for August 1926:

> One day early last spring when I went down to see the progress of the work I found Mr Jones full of enthusiasm about a new scheme for making the hall a palais de danse. Three months later when I saw the main buildings I found that the dance hall idea had been carried out and that the 'Plaza Salon de Danse and Cafe' was to open in September.

It opened amid fierce competition from Maximes and the Marine Gardens but a high standard of music, dancing and formal dress eventually brought success. The main ballroom was on an upper floor with the restaurant between it and the smaller east ballroom on a lower floor. In the main ballroom the male fraternity took up a position on the slightly elevated balcony to survey the flock of city belles, whose only escape was a curt refusal to dance. As the evening developed, couples progressed to the restaurant and then to the east ballroom where the standard of dancing was much higher. For those without a sense of rhythm, the intimate atmosphere and the euphoria of the moment appeared to compensate for the lack of basic skills. Over the years, several well-known bands have played at the Plaza including Lionel Murrey's London Dance Band in the 1920s, Joe Smith and the Uterpians after 1945, and the Colorado under the leadership of George McIntosh. Their repertoire reflected the many changes in dance styles up to the mid-1970s when ballroom dancing ceased to draw large crowds. The Plaza closed after the last waltz on Saturday 1st March 1975, and the building was demolished in 1980. The supermarket built on the site in 1981 has a bronze plaque with the following inscription:

This Safeway Superstore
Now stands on the site of
The Jones Motor House
and
The Plaza Ballroom

When the Plaza opened in 1926, Morningside's main picture house was the Springvalley Cinema which closed in 1938. It was replaced by the very much grander Dominion Cinema opened on 31st January 1938. After serving in the First World War, Captain W. M. Cameron opened the Lyceum Cinema in Slateford Road in 1926; later he decided that his next cinema should be in Morningside. Fortunately, he already had the material, a pink-coloured artificial stone manufactured as Craighall Cast Stone by one of his other business interests. He acquired a site in Newbattle Terrace to the east of Morningside Parish Church Hall, and instructed the famous cinema architect, T. Bowhill Gibson, to draw up plans in the flamboyant Art Deco style of the period. The cinema was completed in only three months. In 1939, at the outbreak of the Second World War, the Dominion, in common with all cinemas in the country, was closed. Fortunately, the compulsory closure had been in existence for only two weeks when Winston Churchill announced in the House of Commons that cinemas should reopen to boost the morale of the people.

Throughout the Second World War and into the period of declining cinema audiences, the Dominion maintained a family atmosphere in its management and its patrons. Complete independence from the film distribution organisations enabled it to control the type and duration of its film programme in a way which was not open to many of its competitors. Large-scale alterations were undertaken in 1972, when two separate cinemas were constructed within the original building. The occasion was marked by a reopening by Moira Shearer on 25th May 1972 with the programme *Cold Turkey* and *On a Clear Day You Can See Forever*. Eight years later, in 1980, further expansion took place to provide a third cinema built into the roof space above the reception area. This commitment to expansion and innovation paid dividends when the Dominion won First Prize out of 1,242 entries in the United Kingdom, in the category 'Comfort and Decor' of the Cinema 1987 Awards. Comfort and decor were still the main criteria a decade later,

The Dominion Cinema, built by Captain W. M. Cameron, and opened on 31st January 1938, is still privately owned by the Cameron family. *Photograph by Derek M. Cameron.*

when major reorganisation of the area, previously used as The Spool Room Restaurant, was undertaken in 1997. Judicious use of the space available created a fourth cinema to seat 60, and a refurbished cafe-bar on two levels – ample evidence that the Dominion still has an appetite for expansion more than sixty years after it was first opened.

The Dominion is still very much a family business: Mrs J. M. Cameron, widow of Captain W. M. Cameron, was Chairman up until the time of her death in 1993; her son Derek M. Cameron is now Chairman; and Mr Cameron's two sons and daughter have come into the business as the third generation of the Cameron family involved in the Dominion. The sons, Michael and Al, are joint Managing Directors, and daughter Lesley is Managing Director of Dominion Property Co. Ltd.

In 1935 Morningside was fortunate to have its very own infantry. A contingent is seen here, at attention, in the back green of No. 49 Falcon Gardens. From left to right: Graham Moonie; his sister Annot Moonie; Myles Crooke; and Dougie. *Courtesy of Graham Moonie.*

The Canny Man's or the Volunteer Arms, a favourite Morningside hostelry, has been in the hands of the Kerr family for more than a century. *Photograph by Phyllis M. Cant.*

Long before the era of the Plaza and the Dominion the old village of Morningside expanded gradually southwards to include several early-nineteenth century cottages and villas in Canaan Lane and Jordan Lane. The village inn, probably dating from before Falcon Hall, stood on the south corner of Canaan Lane and Morningside Road. Originally known as The Volunteers' Rest, or The Rifleman, it later changed its name to The Volunteer Arms or The Canny Man's. At the end of the eighteenth century it was a small single-storey building resembling a cottage which was purchased by James Kerr in 1871. He succeeded in building up a substantial clientèle consisting of local people, the carters and labourers from surrounding farms, and the men of the Edinburgh Volunteers who practised shooting in a field near the Blackford Hill. The present building, under the name of The Volunteer Arms or The Canny Man's, is still in the hands of the Kerr family. A few yards east of The Volunteer Arms, in Canaan Lane, the former police station and fire station still exist, although no longer used for these purposes. They were built in 1893 on two storeys to provide three cells, a muster room, witness room and charge room, in addition to a firemen's room and fire engine house.

This natural development of the village, southwards, was held in check by the presence of the toll-house at Briggs o' Braid, i.e. the bridge over the Jordan Burn. The *Edinburgh and Leith Post Office Directory Map* of 1853 shows the toll-house on the south bank of the Jordan Burn, which, nowadays, runs in a pipe under the small lane to the south of Morningside Post Office. The toll-house appears to have been built around 1852 when the previous toll at Wright's Houses, near the Barclay Church, was abolished. Not unnaturally, this extra financial burden was disliked by those residents of Morningside who lived south of the Jordan Burn, and, for many years, its existence seriously restricted the growth of housing to the south. After road tolls were abolished completely in 1883, Sir John Skelton of the Hermitage of Braid bought the toll-house, had it demolished and re-erected it as a lodge house at the entrance to the Hermitage, where it still stands.

Braid United Presbyterian Church (now Morningside Braid Parish Church) was built slightly to the east of the old toll-house. The

A young lad in Highland dress (not the one who ran behind Lord Gardenstone's horse) with his sister in Canaan Lane in 1935. *Courtesy of Graham Moonie.*

Looking north on Morningside Road, *c.* 1942. Window blinds are very much in evidence on the shop fronts on the sunny side of the street.

congregation, formed in October 1883 under its first minister, the Rev. Walter Brown of Galashiels, first worshipped in a temporary iron church at the north end of Braid Road and Comiston Road on ground now occupied by a red sandstone tenement above the Hermitage Bar. Within two years of the congregation being formed, the building fund had reached £1,140, which enabled the congregation to give serious thought to building a permanent church. The site at the west end of Nile Grove was purchased and the distinguished architect George Washington Browne was employed to draw up plans for a church to seat 750 at a total cost of £5,000. The foundation stone was laid on Saturday 9th October 1886 and the church was opened for public worship on 10th July 1887. The completed building is very different to any other church in Morningside. The simple octagonal shape is enhanced by a half-round portico entrance, supported by pairs of Ionic pillars, above which is a steep-sided pediment, flanked by two open conical towers. Internally, the octagonal shape created an interesting auditorium in which the congregation was arranged around the pulpit, the organ and the choir. The chancel area was greatly improved during extensive renovation work in 1952 by re-siting the organ and choir on the south-east side. The centenary of the opening of the church was marked in 1987 by numerous events and the erection of a small granite stone, and plaque, in the church grounds. Below an engraving of the old iron church is the following inscription:

From 27 January 1883 Braid
(U.P.) Church worshipped in an iron
building, shown above, some 300 yards
south of this site.
The present church, designed by
George Washington Browne, was
opened on 10 July 1887.
We praise thee, O Lord.

10 July 1987

The idea of the stone, erected to mark the church centenary, was given financial support from the Smith family of Morningside in honour of their parents, who were lifelong members of the congregation. After

Braid Church was designed by George Washington Browne and opened on 10th July 1887. It became Morningside Braid Parish Church in 1990 when the congregations of Braid Church and Morningside Parish Church united.

Morningside Parish Church united with Braid Church in 1990, several artefacts from the Parish Church were transferred to the Braid building. Among these is the carved wooden plaque previously at the Parish Church which has now been installed in the vestibule of the new Morningside Braid building:

THIS CHURCH WAS DEDICATED
ON 29TH JULY 1838 BY THE
REV. THOMAS CHALMERS D.D., LL.D.
AT THE DISRUPTION IN 1843 THE MINISTER
THE REV. THOMAS ADDIS WITH A PROPORTION
OF THE CONGREGATION LEFT TO FORM MORNINGSIDE
FREE CHURCH. THE LATTER BECAME IN 1929
MORNINGSIDE HIGH CHURCH OF THE REUNITED CHURCH
OF SCOTLAND. ON 12TH JUNE 1960
THE FORMER MORNINGSIDE PARISH AND MORNINGSIDE
HIGH CONGREGATIONS WERE REUNITED IN THIS CHURCH
UNDER THE REV. FRANK WOOD.

A new plaque, made to match the Morningside Parish plaque, has also

The plaque brought from Morningside Parish Church and now installed in the Morningside Braid building. *Courtesy of Morningside Braid Parish Church. Photograph by W. R. Smith.*

been installed in the vestibule recording the corresponding events for Braid Church:

BRAID U.P. CHURCH, ORIGINALLY
THE IRON KIRK NEAR MORNINGSIDE
STATION, MOVED TO THIS BUILDING IN JULY
1887 UNDER ITS MINISTER, REV. WALTER
BROWN. IN 1929 BRAID CHURCH BECAME A
PART OF THE CHURCH OF SCOTLAND. IN MAY
1990 MORNINGSIDE PARISH CHURCH UNITED WITH
BRAID CHURCH. THE CONGREGATION
OF MORNINGSIDE BRAID PARISH CHURCH WAS
ESTABLISHED IN THIS BUILDING IN SEPTEMBER 1990
REV. JOHN R. WELLS
WAS INDUCTED TO THE CHARGE IN JANUARY 1991.

Unfortunately, it did not prove practical to bring together the various War Memorials which were located in the three churches. However, a composite Book of Remembrance incorporating the names of those who fell in both World Wars, from each church, was produced. The red leather-bound book, with its gold-embossed legend and symbol, is

The new plaque in Morningside Braid Church which matches the Morningside Parish plaque. *Courtesy of Morningside Braid Parish Church. Photograph by W. R. Smith.*

located in a carved oak plinth, situated in the vestibule on the former Morningside Parish Church Communion Table.

After the toll at Briggs o' Braid was abolished, Morningside developed rapidly to the south with Maxwell Street being one of the first streets to be built. In 1884, when Morningside Road Station was opened for passenger traffic, it became the natural focal point of the neighbourhood. Much of the planning for the successful suburban line was undertaken by Thomas Bouch, designer of the ill-fated Tay Bridge, which collapsed with the loss of many lives on 28th December 1879. After the Tay Bridge disaster, Bouch was relieved of his commission on the suburban line, and the final survey was undertaken by George Trimble of Trimble & Peddie. The surviving plans and papers are held by the Scottish Record Office. Sir Thomas Bouch died in October 1880 before the suburban line was opened, and was buried in Dean Cemetery.

When the station opened, a group of Edinburgh businessmen, headed by Colonel Trotter of Mortonhall, decided to build a hotel on the corner of Braid Road and Comiston Road, but when the work was finished there were insufficient funds to complete the enterprise, and the building was converted into tenement flats. A less ambitious scheme, which nevertheless provided the district with its most distinctive landmark, was completed in 1910 when the station clock was presented to the people of Morningside by three local Town Councillors, R. K. Inches, William Inman and William Torrance. The Torrance family owned Torrance's Tea Room, a popular venue on the corner of Comiston Road and Belhaven Terrace. At the west end of Belhaven Terrace, Morningside Cemetery was laid out in 1878 and is the burial place of several eminent persons, including William Cowan, a past President of the Old Edinburgh Club who bequeathed a valuable collection of books and papers on Edinburgh to the City Library; also Alison Cunningham, 'Cummy', Robert Louis Stevenson's nurse; and in much more recent times, Sir Edward Appleton, Principal and Vice-Chancellor of Edinburgh University who died in 1965. Morningside's War Memorial, to those who fell in the First World War, is also located in the cemetery. The tall granite cross, bearing a sword on its north and south faces, stands on an octagonal plinth in the centre of a raised grassy bank in the north-east corner of the graveyard. In 1981 a detailed *Survey of Monumental Inscriptions in Morningside Cemetery* was compiled by members of the Morningside Association headed by Mrs Sheila B. Durham

The station clock was presented to the people of Morningside in 1910 by three local Town Councillors: R. K. Inches; William Inman; and William Torrance. *Photograph by Phyllis M. Cant.*

For several months during 1997–98 the people of Morningside waited patiently for the clock to be returned after it had been taken away for restoration. *Photograph by W. R. Smith.*

On 14th July 1998 'Morningside time' was restored when the City of
Edinburgh Council arranged for the renovated clock to be re-erected on the
traffic island at the south end of Morningside Road.
Photograph by Louise Maguire.

who did much of the early research. This invaluable source of genea-
logical information, in two volumes, copies of which have been
deposited with the National Library of Scotland and Edinburgh City
Library, records all the headstones between 1878 and 1981, indexed,
and divided into categories by occupation, qualification, sculpture etc.

Cluny Parish Church, on the corner of Cluny Gardens and Braid
Road, was formed in 1974 from the union of St Matthew's Parish
Church and South Morningside Parish Church. In October 1886 Hippolyte J. Blanc was employed to draw up plans for St Matthew's Parish
Church; the foundation stone was laid on 1st June 1888 by the Lord
High Commissioner of the General Assembly of the Church of Scotland,
the Earl of Hopetoun; and the opening service was held on 4th May
1890. Within a few years, another elegant church, this time designed
by Rowand Anderson, was built on the north corner of Cluny Drive
and Braid Road, and opened in 1892 as Braid Road Free Church. Shortly
afterwards it was renamed South Morningside Free Church and in 1929
it became South Morningside Church on the union of the United Free

St Matthew's Parish Church was designed by the architect, Hippolyte J. Blanc, and opened on 4th May 1890. In 1974 it became Cluny Parish Church on the union of the congregations of St Matthew's Parish Church and South Morningside Parish Church.

Church and the Established Church. When Cluny Parish Church was formed in 1974 the St Matthew's building was used for worship and the South Morningside building was later converted to Cluny Church Centre.

On the west side of Braid Road, a few yards north of the junction with Comiston Terrace, are 'The Hanging Stanes', Morningside's link with the days of highway robbery. Opposite No. 66 Braid Road, a plaque set into the pavement carries the inscription:

THE HANGING STANES

THOMAS KELLY AND HENRY ORNEIL,
THE LAST TWO HIGHWAYMEN IN SCOTLAND TO BE
EXECUTED, WERE HANGED IN PUBLIC ON 25TH
JANUARY 1815, FROM THE GALLOWS ERECTED ON
THE TWO STANES STILL VISIBLE ON THE SPOT
WHICH WAS WHERE THE ROBBERY TOOK PLACE

1993   PAID FOR BY PUBLIC SUBSCRIPTION

Hector Waugh and his daughter, Alison Waugh, outside the family home at No. 27 Braid Avenue in the summer of 1949. The Pony Lady with the barrel organ was a frequent visitor to Morningside and other suburbs in the 1940s and 1950s. *Courtesy of Alison Waugh.*

On 23rd November 1814 two itinerant Irishmen, Thomas Kelly and Henry Orneil, alias O'Neil, attacked and robbed David Loch, a carter from Biggar, who was on his way on horseback to the city of Edinburgh. The incident occurred near the bridge over the Braid Burn at the entrance to the Hermitage of Braid. In the ensuing scuffle, Loch was dragged from his horse, struck in the face with a pistol and robbed of four one-pound notes, twenty shillings in silver, a two-penny loaf and his spleuchan, or tobacco pouch. Fortunately for David Loch his cries for help were heard by two local men who came to his assistance, and later testified against the two accused in court. At their trial before the Lord Justice Clerk, the Hon. David Boyle, the two men were found guilty and sentenced to be hanged, in the words of the judge, 'not at the ordinary place [the Tolbooth Prison] but on the spot where you robbed and assaulted David Loch, or as near as possible to that spot'. By all accounts, the execution was a major attraction in Edinburgh at the time, *The Edinburgh Evening Courant* reporting that 'we never on any occasion witnessed so great a crowd, who had walked out in a snowstorm the three miles from the High Street'. The two square stones, five inches thick by one metre square, into which the gibbet was fitted, can still be seen, set into the roadway opposite No. 66 Braid Road. Over the years, many eminent writers have been attracted to the story, including Robert Louis Stevenson in *Edinburgh: Picturesque Notes*; Margaret Warrender in *Walks near Edinburgh*; William Mair in *Historic Morningside*; and, most recently, Charles J. Smith in Vol. 2 of *Historic South Edinburgh*.

Craiglea Dairy at No. 98 Comiston Road was run by Mr Peter McKay and his wife Mrs Jane McKay, née Muirhead, from 1930 to 1937. Milk was supplied early each morning by William Wilkie of Comiston Farm and then poured into bottles or cans. The photograph shows Mrs Jane McKay, on the right, and her assistant in the shop *c.* 1934. Among the items for sale were many well-known brands of the day: McVitie & Price's Cheddar Assortment; Carr's Biscuits; Crawford's Rover Assorted; Macfarlane Lang's Gipsy Creams; and Lyon's Chocolate Cream Bars. The bracket for the original gas lighting can be seen to the right of the door. *Courtesy of Mrs Marion C. Wright, née McKay.*

In the 1990s the subject of the hanging stanes was again in the public eye when George S. Russell of Braid Road launched an appeal to have the stones scheduled as Ancient Monuments and properly recorded with an accompanying plaque. The idea caught the imagination of the local community who were supported by Lothian Regional Council, Edinburgh District Council, Historic Scotland, the Cockburn Association, Morningside Association, Morningside Heritage Association and the Community Council. As a result, the commemorative plaque was unveiled by the Right Hon. Lord Ross, the Lord Justice Clerk, at a short ceremony on Saturday 11th September 1993. Among those present was the late John Smith, leader of the Labour Party, who, at that time, lived in Cluny Drive, nearby. John Smith's memorial service, attended by many national and international statesmen, was held on 20th May 1994 at Cluny Parish Church.

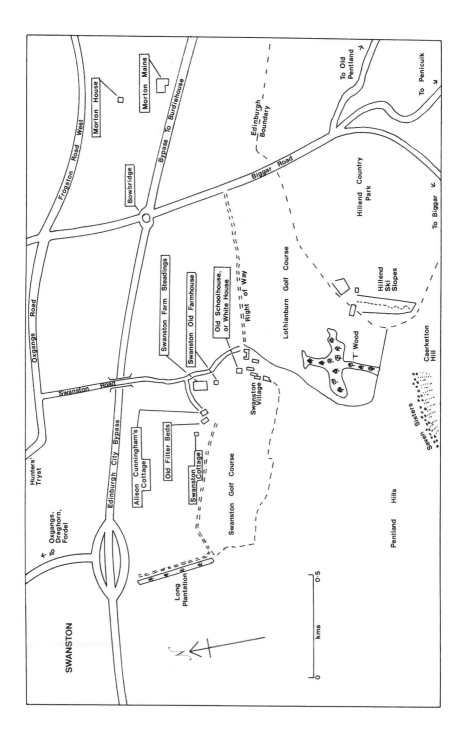

SWANSTON

To Oxgangs,
Dreghorn,
Fordel

Hunters'
Tryst

Oxgangs Road

Frogston Road West

Morton House

Morton Mains

Bowbridge

Bypass To Burdiehouse

Edinburgh Boundary

Edinburgh City Bypass

Swanston Road

Swanston Farm Steadings

Swanston Old Farmhouse

Old Schoolhouse,
or White House

Right of Way

Biggar Road

Hillend Country Park

To Old Pentland

To Penicuik

Alison Cunningham's Cottage

Old Filter Beds

Swanston Cottage

Swanston Village

Lothianburn Golf Course

Hillend Ski Slopes

To Biggar

Long Plantation

Swanston Golf Course

T Wood

Caerketton Hill

Seven Sisters

Pentland Hills

kms

0   0·5

CHAPTER SEVEN

Swanston

Swanston lies close to the southern boundary of Edinburgh, at the base of Caerketton Hill, surrounded by small wooded areas and open farmland. It is one of Edinburgh's most picturesque villages, and is the only one to remain largely unaffected by the spread of suburban development. Ironically, Swanston does not have many of the traditional essentials of village life: there is no church; there has been no school for more than sixty years; there are no shops, pubs, or buses; and there is no village street. Despite this, or perhaps because of this, Swanston exudes the old-world charm of a quiet country village, with whitewashed thatched cottages, one or two larger dwellings, and the old steadings of Swanston Farm, now in domestic and commercial use.

Swanston has played an important part in the development of Edinburgh, and in its reputation abroad. Following lengthy litigation with the local landowner, the springs at Swanston were piped in 1761 to augment Edinburgh's first water supply from Comiston. In the late nineteenth century Swanston Cottage was the summer retreat of Robert Louis Stevenson before his departure to Samoa, and Hunters Tryst, nearby, was the meeting place of the Six Foot Club. The club was formed in 1826 for the promotion of athletics and gymnastics, with membership restricted to persons of at least six feet in height, although exceptions were made for honorary members. Among the many famous literary members were Sir Walter Scott, James Hogg (the Ettrick Shepherd) and J. G. Lockhart (son-in-law and biographer of Sir Walter Scott).

More recently Lothianburn Golf Club and Swanston Golf Club have extended their hold on the lower slopes of the Pentland Hills, and further afield, Hillend Ski Centre is one of the largest artificial slopes in Europe. Hillend Park was gifted to the city by John White, an Edinburgh builder, and was opened to the public by Lord Provost Sir William Sleigh in July 1924. It was designated as a Country Park in 1981 under the Countryside (Scotland) Act of 1967. The first ski-slope was laid out in 1964 with assistance and financial backing from G. Boyd Anderson, an Edinburgh businessman.

About half a mile to the north of the village, the City Bypass creates an obvious barrier between Edinburgh and Pentland Regional Park, designated in 1984, to the south. The Bypass should, therefore, be the southern extent of suburban housing on the south-facing slopes from Oxgangs Road. If this can be achieved, the unique character of Swanston, in a Conservation Area, will be protected well into the twenty-first century.

A view of Swanston from below Oxgangs Road, in 1949, with the Pentland Hills in the background before the ski-slope was constructed. Swanston Farmhouse is hidden by the trees at the south end of Swanston Road. The line of trees in the foreground of the picture was removed for the construction of the City Bypass. *Courtesy of* The Scotsman Publications Ltd.

THE VILLAGE WALK

Swanston village can be reached, either along the right of way from Biggar Road at Lothianburn, or by Swanston Road running south from Oxgangs Road, near Hunters Tryst. The old Swanston Road, formerly little more than a cart track, formed the boundary between what was Easter and Wester Swanston. Easter Swanston belonged to the Ross family from the fifteenth century and passed to Henry Trotter of Mortonhall in 1749. Wester Swanston belonged to Sir John Cockburn in 1462, thereafter to the Foulis family of Colinton in 1538, and finally to the Trotters of Mortonhall in 1670. In addition to Easter and Wester Swanston there were the small, but important, Temple Lands, the exact location of which is now uncertain. Charles J. Smith in *Historic South Edinburgh* states that 'the name is believed to have originated with the Templars, or Knights of the Temple, an association of men whose vows united those of monks with those of knights, and whose object was to protect pilgrims on visits to the Holy Land'. They settled at Temple in Midlothian in the twelfth century. Their association with Swanston is confirmed in a charter of James VI, dated 1614, in which all the Templars' possessions in Scotland are listed, including a reference to 'terras templarias de Swaistoun possessas'.

Today Swanston Road follows approximately the same line as the earlier road but has been greatly widened on the section between Oxgangs Road and the bridge over the City Bypass. On the south side of the bridge the road continues down into the hollow, where the Swanston Burn has been realigned, before rising again towards the steadings of Swanston Farm. Immediately past the square courtyard and grieve's cottage, there is a newer house built in 1948 for the greenkeeper at Swanston Golf Club, but no longer used for that purpose. The house was named Rathillet by the founder of the club, Miss Margaret Carswell, whose family came from a farm near the village of Rathillet in Fife. Swanston Golf Clubhouse lies to the right of the car park which was created from part of the garden ground of the former Swanston farmhouse. This L-plan building, dating from the early eighteenth century, has not always been maintained to the standard expected of a category B listed building. After its use as a farmhouse was discontinued in 1959 it provided accommodation for casual farm labourers at the harvest and potato-lifting seasons. During this period its condition deteriorated greatly despite protests from the Cockburn Association. Following a serious fire in 1984 it was acquired by a firm of builders who renovated the entire property and formed three distinctive houses around a U-shaped courtyard. The general character of the surrounding policies was maintained, albeit at some temporary cost to lawns and shrubs The main part of the old farmhouse with the crowstepped gables was completely refurbished to create an elegant modern house on three floors without losing the character of the eighteenth-century stonework. Similar renovation was completed on the smaller adjacent house to the south, and the original cottage, which formed the east wing, was extended to create a larger house. In 1986, when the garden was being renovated, the remains of an old tennis court was discovered on a level piece of ground to the north-west of the house.

To the south-east of the farmhouse a half-square of stone cottages with slated roofs and ornamental chimney pots looks onto a small communal green. The cottages were originally built for farm workers in the late nineteenth century. The former residents recalled when water

Swanston Farmhouse dates from the early eighteenth century. After a serious fire in 1984 it was completely renovated and divided into three distinctive houses around a U-shaped courtyard. *Courtesy of A. W. Brotchie.*

THE FARM HOUSE SWANSTON J.P.

was first installed in 1934 and electricity in 1949. About fifteen men were employed to work a thousand acres of sheep, cattle and arable farming. Wages were around twenty-five shillings per week (£1.25p) depending upon seniority, with the 'first man' receiving an extra shilling per week for the responsibility of ensuring that the others got out of their beds and into the fields by the appointed hour. Nine Clydesdale or Belgian horses were used on the land, each of the four pairs kept by an experienced hand, and the single horse looked after by the apprentice, who did all the fetching and carrying. The first man usually drove a pair of white horses which, when working in the fields early in the morning, were more easily seen by the farmer from his vantage point in the farmhouse.

The White House, or Schoolhouse, frequently mistaken for Swanston

The White House, in 1987, an elegant private dwelling in its own grounds, formerly the schoolhouse for children travelling from Bowbridge, Lothianburn, Fordel and Dreghorn. In 1992 it was renamed, appropriately, The Old Schoolhouse.

Cottage, lies a hundred yards to the west of the farm cottages, surrounded by a large country garden through which flows the Swanston
Burn. This large, two-storey house of uncertain date was formerly the
village schoolhouse for children travelling as far afield as Bowbridge,
Lothianburn, Comiston House, Fordel and Dreghorn. Children from
ages five to fourteen were put into age groups rather than same-age
classes, which posed particular problems for the teachers, Miss Graham
and later Mrs Boyd. When the school closed in 1931 the property was
bought by Mr and Mrs Boyd and the old schoolroom became a
fashionable dining room. In 1992 it was renamed, appropriately, the
Old Schoolhouse.

Slightly further up the hill from the White House the rough pathway
opens out onto a well-tended undulating green, with Lothianburn Golf
Course to the east, and Swanston Golf Course to the west. At the end
of the Second World War this part of Swanston consisted of very basic
early eighteenth-century cottages with earth floors and no water or
electricity. A particularly bad winter in 1947 left forty villagers virtually
cut off by huge snowdrifts, bread and other supplies being brought in
by a horse-drawn snow plough from Oxgangs Road. Although high-
voltage electricity pylons hummed almost overhead the houses were
dependent upon oil for heating and cooking. In May 1949 a petition
was directed to the South East of Scotland Electricity Board on behalf
of Swanston Farm, Swanston Cottage, the Schoolhouse and Swanston
Golf Club which resulted in electricity being installed in the village. By
1954, however, the thatched cottages at the top end of the village had
fallen into a serious state of disrepair, and many of those which were
habitable were used only as holiday cottages. In 1956 an ambitious
scheme, originally estimated at £17,000, was put forward by the City
Architect for conversion of nine old cottages into seven renovated
dwellings, and associated landscaping. Work progressed slowly, the
specialised job of thatching being done by John Brough of Auchter-
muchty. By 1960 the eventual cost of renovation was nearer to £26,000.
Edinburgh Corporation then invited tenders from more than ninety
eager applicants to rent one of the completed houses. The successful
few, some of whom subsequently bought their cottage under recent
legislation, secured a beautifully restored eighteenth-century cottage on
a three-year lease, the conditions of which prohibited the use of external
television aerials, and the sale or display of souvenirs, postcards or

Thatched cottages, beautifully restored, in a quiet rural setting in the heart of Swanston village.

refreshments. After several years of neglect Swanston once again earned Stevenson's description of almost a century earlier – though without the qualification in parenthesis:

> The hamlet ... consists of a few cottages on a green beside a burn. Some of them (a strange thing in Scotland) are models of internal neatness; the beds adorned with patch, the shelves arrayed with willow-pattern plates, the floors and tables bright with scrubbing or pipe-clay, and the very kettle polished like silver.

At the highest point of the green there is a teak bench with the following inscription to another well-known poet and novelist:

> To the memory of Edwin Muir 1887–1959
> Poet, Novelist, Essayist, Teacher.
> This seat is given by his friends to
> the village of Swanston where the poet
> liked to linger and meditate.

In May 1962 the seat was handed over by Lord Guthrie, Senator of the College of Justice, and chairman of the Committee of Trustees of the Edwin Muir Memorial Fund, and accepted by Lord Provost Sir

John Greig Dunbar. Within a few yards there is another commemorative bench to one of Swanston's former residents:

HAPPY MEMORIES OF
JOHN ROE
1915–1995

I LIFT MY EYES
TO THE QUIET HILLS
TO A CALM THAT IS MINE TO SHARE

From the gate at the top of the green the pathway rises steeply towards the distinctive scree slopes of the Seven Sisters on Caerketton Hill. To the east is the T wood laid out by Henry Trotter of Mortonhall in 1766. Although seen as T-shaped from Edinburgh, it is actually in the form of a Maltese cross, which detracts from the argument that the wood was planted by Trotter ('T' for Trotter?) to assert dominion over water rights. An Act of Parliament of 1758 permitted Edinburgh Corporation to use spring water from Swanston to increase the public water supply from Comiston Springs. The Act provided for compensation and procedures for potential disputes. As anticipated, Henry Trotter objected, saying that he required the water for his own use, and that in any case the water would hardly be needed if the Comiston pipes did not leak so badly. As the matter could not be resolved, the case went to the Sheriff Court, which ruled in favour of Edinburgh Corporation. Trotter appealed, firstly to the Court of Session, and then to the House of Lords in May 1760, when he was again unsuccessful. Edinburgh Corporation proceeded with the work of tapping the fresh clear water from numerous springs, and a water-house was constructed in 1761, a few hundred yards to the west of the village. The inscription on the lintel stone, giving the date and the name of the Lord Provost, can still be seen:

EDINBURGH
GEORGIUS LIND PRAEFECTUS
ANNO MDCCLXI

Three slow sand filter beds were later constructed of brick with slated roofs to collect and purify the water from several sources. A system of stopcocks allowed the supply to be switched between each of the three beds to allow for cleaning the sand. This was brought out manually and washed in a separate pond with the water flow reversed in order to float the impurities to the surface. Nearby is the water engineer's cottage. Its curious lintel stone with the inscription 1880 AC 1893 opens another chapter in the history of Swanston.

SWANSTON COTTAGE AND R.L.S.

After the water-house was constructed in 1761 the city fathers decided that additional accommodation was needed as a general meeting place. The small single-storey thatched cottage which they built to the north-west is described by Robert Louis Stevenson in *Edinburgh: Picturesque Notes:*

> After they had built their water-house and laid their pipes, it occurred to them that the place was suitable for junketing. Once entertained, with jovial magistrates and public funds, the idea led speedily to accomplishment; and Edinburgh could soon boast of a municipal Pleasure House. The dell was turned into a garden; and on the knoll that shelters it from the plain and the sea winds, they built a cottage looking to the hills.

Swanston Cottage, in 1987, the summer residence of R.L.S. from 1867 to 1880, setting for *St Ives* and the inspiration for many of Stevenson's verses. *Photograph by Phyllis M. Cant.*

The Cottage was greatly enlarged around 1835 when the magistrates added a second storey and replaced the thatch with slate. Bow windows were built out at the front and a single-storey addition was constructed to the east. Fothergill, in *Stones and Curiosities of Edinburgh and Neighbourhood*, describes and illustrates several gargoyles and finials brought to Swanston Cottage from St. Giles Cathedral during the extensive alterations by William Burn the architect in 1830. These were used to embellish the roof of the east extension and the high stone wall beside the quarry garden. By far the most interesting era, however, began at Whitsunday 1867 when Thomas Stevenson, father of Robert Louis Stevenson, took the tenancy of the house as a summer retreat. Little did he know that Swanston Cottage was to become the romantic setting and inspiration for so many of Robert Louis Stevenson's poems and novels.

Robert Lewis Balfour Stevenson was born in Edinburgh on 13th November 1850. On his father's side the family had a long tradition as highly specialised engineers. Louis' grandfather, Robert Stevenson, had built the Bell Rock Lighthouse and Louis' father had continued the family tradition. Louis' mother was Margaret Balfour of the Balfours of Pilrig, whose father was the Rev. Lewis Balfour of Colinton Parish Church. When the Stevensons married on 28th August 1848 they set up house at No. 8 Howard Place. After a short stay at No. 1 Inverleith Terrace (now renumbered 9) they moved to No. 17 Heriot Row which was their main residence during the tenancy of Swanston Cottage. Early in Stevenson's life the name Balfour was dropped and the spelling was altered from Lewis to Louis apparently on account of his father's aversion to a Radical politician named Lewis. As a young child, and throughout his short life, Louis was dogged by ill health which eventually hastened his departure from Edinburgh. His sleepless nights and anxious days would have seemed infinitely longer, however, had it not been for the endless support and encouragement given by his nurse Alison Cunningham. Cummy, as she became known, looked after Stevenson from an early age and undoubtedly played a very important and influential role in his life. In gratitude, and in recalling these early days, Stevenson dedicated to her *A Child's Garden of Verses*, published in 1884:

> For the long nights you lay awake
> And watched for my unworthy sake;

Robert Louis Stevenson, born 13th November 1850, qualified as an advocate in 1875, but instead of going into practice he followed his first ambition to become an author. *Photograph from* Robert Louis Stevenson's Edinburgh Days.

ALISON CUNNINGHAM
R.L. STEVENSON'S NURSE "CUMMY"

KNOX SERIES

Stevenson's nurse, Alison Cunningham, or 'Cummy', to whom he dedicated
A Child's Garden of Verses.

For your most comfortable hand
That led me through the uneven land:
For all the story books you read:
For all the pains you comforted:
For all you pitied, for all you bore,
In sad and happy days of yore:-
My second Mother, my first Wife,
The angel of my infant life-
From the sick child now well and old,
Take, nurse, the little book you hold.

Although ill health was certainly a factor in Stevenson's life, it did not confine him to a life of inaction. It was his father's forlorn hope that he would follow in the family footsteps and become an eminent civil engineer, but after a period of study at Edinburgh University, it was clear that no bridges would be built. Stevenson's one ambition was to become a writer. In a final bid to provide his son with a 'respectable' profession, Mr Stevenson persuaded Louis to study law, in which he qualified as an advocate in 1875. Instead of going into practice he went to France, a journey which provided the inspiration for *An Inland Voyage* and *Travels with a Donkey*. By then Stevenson knew what Cummy had probably always known – that 'her boy' would become a famous author.

Stevenson's parents held the tenancy of Swanston Cottage from 1867 to 1880, during which time Stevenson made frequent use of this quiet country retreat. Whilst at Swanston he formed a lasting friendship with John Tod, the 'Roarin' Shepherd', and Robert Young, the gardener, both of whom unconsciously provided inspiration and dialogue for later novels. In *St. Ives* Stevenson's description of the drovers owes much to his long conversations with John Tod, and Swanston Cottage is the place of safety in which the French prisoner of war found shelter after his escape from Edinburgh Castle. From his bedroom window on the upper storey, Stevenson looked out over Caerketton and Allermuir which inspired so many of his verses and poems.

These timeless days were numbered. In 1880 the Stevensons gave up their tenancy of the Cottage and on 19th May Stevenson was married in America. He returned to Edinburgh in August of that year when his father was instrumental in persuading him to try for the Chair of

Constitutional Law and Constitutional History at Edinburgh University, but he was unsuccessful. He spent the following years in the Riviera and in Bournemouth but when his father died in May 1887 Stevenson visited Edinburgh for the last time. Soon after, he left for America and later settled in Samoa where Swanston was never far from his thoughts:

> I gang nae mair where aince I gaed,
> By Buckstane, Fairmilehead or Braid,
> But far frae Kirk and Toon,
> Oh, still ayont the muckle sea,
> Still are ye dear, and dear to me,
> Auld Reekie, still and on.

Stevenson died at Vailima, Samoa on 3rd December 1894 at the age of forty-four. His mother was devastated 'to weep the eyes that should have wept for me'. Cummy, his second mother, first wife and only nurse, was heartbroken. She had remained at Swanston with her brother who was the waterman, after the Stevensons had left in 1880, and had corresponded with Louis for several years. In 1893 she left for No. 23 Balcarres Street in Morningside. Towards the end of her life she lived with her cousin at Comiston Place where she died on 21st July 1913 at the age of ninety-one, and was buried in Morningside Cemetery.

After the Stevenson era, Swanston Cottage was occupied for a time by Dr Taylor of Edinburgh and later by Lord Guthrie, Senator of the College of Justice. Today the Cottage is privately owned, but there are numerous links with earlier days. On the central upper window-sill is chiselled '1867 RLS 1880', and on the waterman's cottage the lintel, already referred to, commemorates occupation by Alison Cunningham, or Cummy, '1880 AC 1893'.

LOTHIANBURN GOLF CLUB; SWANSTON GOLF CLUB AND MISS MARGARET CARSWELL

Lothianburn Golf Course occupies several acres of ground on the lower slopes of Caerketton Hill, bounded on the north by the right of way to Swanston, on the south by Hillend Park, on the east by Biggar Road, and on the west by Swanston Burn. The idea of a club was first mooted at a meeting of interested parties, under the chairmanship of John Cunningham, on Wednesday 19th July 1893 at No. 5 St Andrew Square.

This old thatched cottage, photographed at Lothianburn *c.* 1911, was used for a while by the greenkeeper of Lothianburn Golf Club. The clubhouse can be seen on the left of the picture.

Among those who attended was Gavin Jack, the tenant farmer at Swanston Farm. Shortly thereafter, the first nine-hole course was laid out mainly by one of Gavin Jack's employees, William Laidlaw, who later became the club's first greenkeeper. In those days Lothianburn appeared to be very much further out of town than it is now. Intimation of the club's first competition stated on specially prepared postcards that 'brakes will leave Morningside Station ... and refreshments will be obtained on the ground'. A steel and timber clubhouse was built three years after the club opened, and in May 1899 the course was extended to eighteen holes, played over 3,844 yards. The first idea for a clubhouse was to utilise the old thatched cottage near the gate to the right of way leading to Swanston village. The main part of the cottage

Tommy Armour, the Edinburgh golfer, and a member of Lothianburn Golf
Club, was winner of the British Open, the United States Open and the
P.G.A. titles in the 1920s and 1930s. *Courtesy of* The Scotsman Publications
Ltd.

was to be the greenkeeper's house and a new storey was to be built for the clubrooms. However, this plan was abandoned in favour of retaining the cottage as the greenkeeper's house only, and building a new modest clubhouse which was opened on 3rd October 1896. Further extensions were built in 1901 but it was not until 1909 that a permanent, substantial building was erected by James Miller of Morningside, and opened by Major Trotter on 24th September 1910.

In 1907 ladies were admitted as temporary members, an experiment which appears to have gained the members' approval. A resolution was passed in 1909 to admit lady members up to a maximum of fifty, the first two applicants being Beatrice Runciman and Norah McLachlan. The club's early heyday was between the First and Second World Wars. In 1928 the course was extensively altered by the famous golf professional, James Braid, to take in ground towards Swanston village and the T wood, and in 1931 the club's most renowned player, Tommy Armour, won the British Open Championship at Carnoustie. In keeping with its proximity to the village, Lothianburn has given some of the holes names associated with Stevenson, namely Seven Sisters, Swanston and St Ives.

In more recent years, increased club membership has required further improvements to the clubhouse facilities. On 4th October 1976 a large extension was opened, costing £28,000, which included new ladies' locker rooms and a new lounge area. Further expenditure in the 1990s, totalling £180,000, provided new locker rooms for gents and juniors, a professional's shop and a secretary's office. The centenary in 1993 was marked by the publication of the club's history, *Lothianburn Golf Club Centenary 1893–1993*, in which the author, William Pritchard, O.B.E., provides a wealth of detail about the formation of the club, its principal players, and its development over the years.

Swanston Golf Club is also laid out on the lower slopes of Caerketton Hill, to the west of the village, the first hole, appropriately named R.L.S., running parallel to the garden of Swanston Cottage. The club was formed in 1927 by Miss Margaret Carswell who was also a prominent member of the Edinburgh Women's Athletic Club. Finding it almost impossible to obtain sufficient places for ladies in local golf clubs (presumably including Lothianburn who had admitted lady members since 1907), Miss Carswell decided to found and construct her own course, solely for the use of female members. Her commitment to a ladies-only club did not, however, influence her choice of employee. Following an earlier meeting with Herbert More at the Merchants of Edinburgh Golf Club at Craiglockhart, Miss Carswell succeeded in engaging him for the job of greenkeeper. A lease of land was obtained from Mr Jack at Swanston Farm and Miss Carswell, assisted by Herbert More, proceeded to lay out a nine-hole course. True to her original concept, Miss Carswell insisted that membership be confined to ladies only, but she eventually came under pressure from her own membership to relax the rule in favour of their own male acquaintances, who also happened to be interested in the game of golf. It was a decision she came to regret, although the increased membership and income enabled the club to extend the course to eighteen holes in the late 1920s, and to build a pavilion in 1935 to replace the rather rudimentary accommodation in one of the old thatched cottages in the village. By 1947 the total membership had risen to four hundred, with men outnumbering ladies by three to one.

The club celebrated its Silver Jubilee on 13th October 1952 when Miss Carswell presented a teak seat (now in the garden of Rathillet in

Miss Margaret Carswell of Swanston Golf Club about to driven off on her tour of inspection of the course which she laid out in 1927. *Courtesy of Jim and Ellen McLagan.*

Edinburgh City Bypass, looking east, near the Lothianburn Junction, in 1999.

Swanston) to Herbert More to mark his long service as greenkeeper. In many ways, however, the 1950s and 1960s were dominated by constant clashes between Miss Carswell's original ideals for the club and the aspirations of the younger, male-dominated committee. As owner and founder of the club she dominated committee meetings, and even in advancing years her control of the club never waned. When well over eighty years of age she purchased a mini-tractor and trailer and was driven around the course by a lady member to inspect the fairways and the condition of the greens.

The club has moved away from its original concept, remembered now by only a few senior members. At the present day there are approximately 550 full members, male and female.

Margaret Carswell was obviously a person of considerable ambition and energy whose interests extended far beyond Swanston Golf Club. In her own characteristically blunt words: 'I was feeling rather bored with the world in general and myself in particular so I answered an advertisement in a newspaper'. The advertisement had been inserted by Mr Stuart Morrow, an American, who was looking for someone to start a Soroptimist Club in Edinburgh, similar to the many existing clubs in the United States. Miss Carswell called together several professional and business women, and the first meeting of the club was held on 29th November 1927 with twenty-six members. Ethel de la Cour was elected President, an honour which was bestowed on many able successors, including Miss C. Fraser Lee, headmistress of St Trinneans School in the Grange and later Park Road. One of the Soroptimists' most interesting rules – subsequently relaxed – was to admit only new members whose profession or occupation was not already represented, Miss Carswell being admitted as a Golf Club Proprietrix.

The Soroptimist Club of Edinburgh under its motto 'Looking Further' is part of the worldwide Soroptimists International and has been involved in a great variety of charitable works and links of friendship. A small booklet, giving details of the club and its activities, was published in 1977 at the time of the Golden Jubilee.

Suggestions for Further Reading

GENERAL

Author	Title	Year of Publication
Anon	*The Lord Provosts of Edinburgh 1296–1932*	1932
Birrell, J. F.	*An Edinburgh Alphabet*	1980
Colston, James	*Edinburgh & District Water Supply*	1890
Fothergill, George A.	*Stones & Curiosities of Edinburgh and Neighbourhood*	1910
Geddie, John	*The Fringes of Edinburgh*	1926
Gifford, John McWilliam, Colin and Walker, David	*The Buildings of Scotland: Edinburgh*	1984
Grant, James	*Old & New Edinburgh*	1882
Harris, Stuart	*The Place Names of Edinburgh*	1996
Hunter, D. L. G.	*Edinburgh's Transport*	1964
McKean, Charles	*Edinburgh: An Illustrated Architectural Guide*	1992
Mullay, Sandy	*The Edinburgh Encyclopaedia*	1996
Royal Commission on the Ancient and Historical Monuments of Scotland	*The City of Edinburgh*	1951
Thomas, Brendon	*The Last Picture Shows: Edinburgh*	1984
Turnbull, Michael	*Edinburgh Portraits*	1987
Wallace, Joyce M.	*The Historic Houses of Edinburgh*	1998
Various	*The Book of the Old Edinburgh Club*	1908 to date
Various	*The Streets of Edinburgh*	1984
Warrender, Margaret	*Walks near Edinburgh*	1895

COLINTON

Colinton Amenity Association		
	Colinton: Seven Walks	1985
Geddie, John	*The Home Country of R.L.Stevenson*	1898
Gladstone-Millar, Lynne		
	The Colinton Story	1994
Murray, Thomas	*Biographical Annals of the Parish of Colinton*	1863
Shankie, David	*The Parish of Colinton*	1902
Steuart, James	*Notes for a History of Colinton Parish*	1938
Stewart, Wendy	*An Act of Faith*	1989
Various	*Colinton Parish Church*	1986
Various	*Portrait of a Parish*	1968

GILMERTON

Geddie, John	*The Fringes of Edinburgh*	1926
Good, George	*Liberton in Ancient and Modern Times*	1893
Peckham, Rev. Dr Colin		
	The New Faith Mission Bible College	1994
Skinner, Rev. Donald M.	*Historic Gilmerton*	1964
Speedy, Tom	*Craigmillar and its Environs*	1892

JUNIPER GREEN

Geddie, John	*The Home Country of R.L.Stevenson*	1898
Jamieson, Stanley (ed:)		
	The Water of Leith	1984
Scottish Women's Rural Institute	*Village History Book*	1966
Shankie, David	*Parish of Colinton*	1902
Tweedie, John	*A Water of Leith Walk*	1974

LIBERTON

Ferenbach, Rev. Campbell	*Annals of Liberton*	1975
Finlayson, Charles P.	*Clement Litill and his Library*	1980
Fothergill, George A.	*Stones & Curiosities of Edinburgh and Neighbourhood*	1910
Good, George	*Liberton in Ancient and Modern Times*	1893
Goodfellow, James	*The Print of his Shoe*	1906
Speedy, Tom	*Craigmillar and its Environs*	1892
Speedy, Tom	*The Election of a Minister at Liberton*	1898

LONGSTONE & SLATEFORD

Baird, Hugh	*Report on the Proposed Edinburgh and Glasgow Union Canal*	1813
Craig, George	*Building Stones used in Edinburgh*	1892
Geddie, John	*The Home Country of R.L.Stevenson*	1898
Harris, Stuart	*Parish in the Past*	1971
Jamieson, Stanley (ed:)	*The Water of Leith*	1984
Stevenson, Drummond	*Memories*	1962
Tweedie, John	*A Water of Leith Walk*	1974
Various	*A. & J. Macnab, A Company History*	1960

MORNINGSIDE

Cochrane, Robert	*Memories of Morningside: About St. Matthew's Morningside*	1906
Davies, Rev. Roderick G. and Pollock, Rev. A.	*Morningside Congregational Church 1887–1937*	1937
Durham, Sheila B. and others	*Survey of Monumental Inscriptions: Morningside Cemetery*	1981

Eddington, Alexander	*North Morningside Church*	1930
Findlay, H.J.	*South Morningside Church of Scotland: A Jubilee Retrospect 1889–1939*	1939
Gowans, John Stuart	*Morningside Parish Church*	1912
Gray, John G.	*The South Side Story*	1962
Littlefair, N. J.	*Christ Church Morningside 1876–1976*	1976
Mair, William	*Historic Morningside*	1947
Mitchell, Alexander	*The Story of Braid Church 1883–1933*	1933
Skelton, Harold	*History of Christ Church Morningside*	1955
Smith, Charles J.	*Historic South Edinburgh* Vol. 1	1978
	Vol. 2	1979
	Vol. 3	1986
	Vol. 4	1988
Smith, Charles J.	*Morningside*	1992
Various	*The Story of Braid Church 1883–1983*	1983
—	*Morningside Parish Church*	1907
—	*St Peter's Edinburgh Golden Jubilee Brochure 1907–1957*	1957

SWANSTON

Balfour, Graham	*The Life of Robert Louis Stevenson*	1913
Fothergill, George A.	*Stones & Curiosities of Edinburgh and Neighbourhood*	1910
Pritchard, William	*Lothianburn Golf Club Centenary 1893–1993*	1993
Simpson, E.Blantyre	*Robert Louis Stevenson's Edinburgh Days*	1914
Smith, Charles J.	*Historic South Edinburgh Vol. 2*	1979
Stevenson, Robert Louis		
	Edinburgh: Picturesque Notes	1910
Various	*Soroptimist International of Edinburgh 1927–1977*	1977
Watt, Lachlan Maclean	*The Hills of Home*	1913

Index

Note: page references in *italics* refer to illustrations